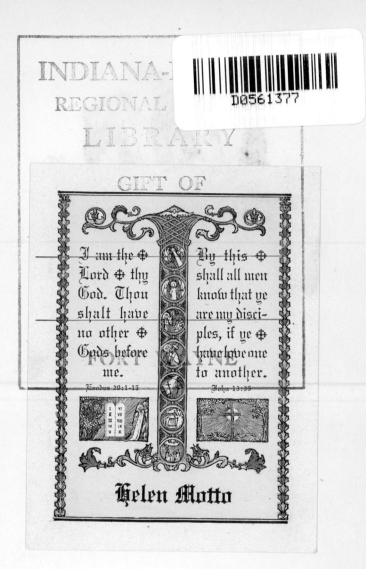

THE STRUGGLE OF THE SOUL

THE MACMILLAN COMPANY
NEW YORK · CHICAGO
DALLAS · ATLANTA · SAN FRANCISCO
LONDON · MANILA

IN CANADA
BRETT-MACMILLAN LTD.
GALT, ONTARIO

THE
STRUGGLE
OF THE
SOUL

Lewis Joseph Sherrill

UNION THEOLOGICAL SEMINARY
NEW YORK, N. Y.

New York: 1959

THE MACMILLAN COMPANY

Ninth Printing 1959

Acknowledgment is made to the following for the use of quoted material:
Abingdon-Cokesbury Press for *Older
People and the Church* by Maves and
Cedarleaf (copyright 1949 by Pierce and
Smith); Princeton University Press for
The Sickness Unto Death by Kierkegaard (copyright 1941); The International Council of Religious Education,
owner of the copyright, for four passages
from the *American Standard Version of
the Bible* (copyright 1929).

to
John Scott Sherrill

Foreword

THIS BOOK is an attempt to trace the religious development of the individual, through the ordinary crises of common life, from infancy to old age. Studies of religious development at particular stages of life are now abundant, but in proportion as these studies multiply we need the more urgently to consider the *entire* life span in its religious aspect.

Such an undertaking, however, requires the choice of a guiding thread, and then the determined exclusion of much that is important, but secondary to the main line of thought. The guiding thread chosen for this purpose is *the dynamic self as it encounters God at the various stages of human life* and responds perhaps by outgoing faith; or perhaps by shrinking back in a self-protecting compromise, or even in full rejection; or perhaps by passing on without knowing it has met God at all.

It can hardly be expected that one author, much less one small volume, can do justice to a subject of such scope and intricacy, but the most which one can ask is that the treatment be judged more by what it contains than by what it omits.

This material, in substance, was delivered as the Smyth Lectures in the presence of the faculty and students of Columbia Theological Seminary, Decatur, Georgia, in May of 1950. Mrs. Sherrill and I feel ourselves under lasting obligation for the warm hospitality extended to us by the members of the faculty and their wives, and especially by President and Mrs. J. McDowell

Richards. I owe particular thanks to Professor Felix B. Geer for his helpful suggestions in connection with certain theological aspects of the material.

To my secretary, Dorothy Hollis, I wish to express hearty appreciation for her help in finding, assembling, and preparing the materials both for the lectures and then for publication.

To my wife, Helen Hardwicke Sherrill, once more I express my profound indebtedness for her knowledge, insight, and suggestions.

Lewis J. Sherrill

Union Theological Seminary
New York City
July, 1950

Contents

CHAPTER ONE

The Struggle of the Soul

THE INDIVIDUAL in the present world is caught between two fires.

On the one hand modern civilization requires that the individual be a person of extraordinary strength if he is to thrive in the midst of that civilization. For in proportion as our civilization grows more complicated, more difficult to understand, and more resistant to rational control, to that extent the individual is the harder put to it to find or make his place in society as a self-respecting personality. And in proportion as the pressures upon modern living grow more numerous and more disturbing, the individual is threatened or even undermined at every soft spot which he carries in his make-up as a person. In a word, modern civilization demands character marked by a high degree of strength and maturity in those who would survive it.

And yet, on the other hand, modern society is producing, in vast numbers, persons who are rendered deficient because they cannot achieve precisely that kind of strength and maturity which our civilization demands. Instead, while the civilization is requiring one thing in the character of men, the society out of which that civilization has arisen tends to produce the very opposite in the character of men.

Moreover, this disparity between the demands *upon* human character and the sufficiency *of* human character, seems to be growing steadily as we advance further into our century. Everyone knows only too well that we live in a time of trouble; harassed by uncertainty, heartbreak, and despair. And "the end is not yet." But meanwhile, as the demands upon human life mount and as the sufficiency of human life dwindles, we catch sight of a growing mass of the neurotic, the insane, the dependent, the blighted, and the untimely dead; while we hear the fear more and more often expressed that the night of western civilization has already set in.

In this time of trouble many, to whom religion has been outside the bounds of personal experience, have sought to find reasonable grounds for hope, only to discover, sometimes to their frank surprise, that their quest has brought them face to face with a Reality which they recognize as God, but a God with whom they do not know how to deal. Others are discovering that religion, as they know it, is not sufficient for the new demands which life is placing upon them. Still others, already at home in the religious life, are finding in religion greater resources than they have ever known before, and are drawing more deeply upon these resources in their day of need. When all such facts are put together and carefully examined, there is much to justify those who say that we are in a time of turning to God.

But man's turning to God may prove to be only one side of something whose other side has an even greater significance. Is it possible that God is now confronting man, in this modern world, with deeper demand and with more hopeful promise than any of us has been able as yet to apprehend? Here again there is much to lead one to believe that this may be so.

THE HUMAN CAREER

But the time of trouble and the human need vary greatly in their meaning to a given individual. This wide variation in meaning depends partly on the time in one's life when he encounters trouble or feels need; and it depends partly on what he has already become

by the time of some fresh encounter. This being so, one's turning to God, or his not turning to God, has an equally wide range
of meaning. And by the same token the inner meaning of religion
to the individual varies just as greatly. While this is always true,
it takes on especial significance when the sense of trouble is wide-
spread and the sense of need deep.

In view of such considerations there seems to be a fresh need
to examine the career of the human self in the modern world, with
his religious development especially in mind. Accordingly, we
propose in this book to follow the career of the human self as it
passes through certain major stages, or types of experience, during
the journey from the beginning to the end of life.

In succeeding chapters we shall take up five of these major
stages and consider them one at a time. But in this chapter we
shall present certain considerations which have to do with the
whole life span at any stage, rather than at one particular stage.

THE MEANING OF LIFE

At the outset we must reckon with the fact that life itself does
not have the same meaning to all who live it. The meanings which
men see in life are vastly varied, they are complex, and they are
subtle. So true is this that it is man's custom, of ancient standing,
to sum up these meanings in apt symbolic terms. Any attempt to
list these symbolic terms for life as a whole would soon yield a
long catalogue of familiar expressions. Who has not heard say
that life is a cloud, or a shadow, or a pain, or a gamble, or a journey, or a dizzy ride on a flywheel, or any other one of a thousand
such terms which light up a man's inner landscape in one quick,
revealing flash?

But wide as the variety of terms is, we can get a fair idea of the
range of meanings which people read into their own lives if we
take three symbolic terms for life as a whole, which are very common. These are the treadmill, the saga, and the pilgrimage.

THE TREADMILL

"Treadmill" is but one of a host of symbolical terms to express the same general but dismal feeling toward life—that it has no meaning. Some of these terms emphasize the monotony of living, as when it is said that life is a squirrel cage, or a weary grind, or an assembly line with a speed up. Other terms refer to excitement which has no meaning except that it breaks monotony and gives a thrill, as when people speak of "the Jazz age." Still others embody in one pithy phrase the notion of a blight which has overtaken something potentially fair and lovely; thus, life is a wasteland, or a desert.

The experience of life as a treadmill is so prominent a part of modern existence that we must reserve this subject for more extended consideration in a later chapter. Here we shall only say that life as a treadmill is virtually all of life that is known by unnumbered millions in the drafted armies, the navies, the mines, the factories, and the businesses of our century. In a word, the external features which characterize modern civilization have the peculiar quality of drying up the souls of the myriads of little people who carry that civilization forward on their backs.

THE SAGA

A second view of life is reflected in the saga, or epic, beloved of men from time immemorial. The saga tells the tale of an individual, or perhaps of a family, and traces the story through innumerable hardships and dangers to whatever end there is that awaits the hero. It is a chronicle of vicissitudes and exploits, and it takes on its peculiar quality from the fact that *it lifts the heroism and glamour of life to a poetic level.*

Thus the saga rises above the treadmill by exalting the distinctively human qualities which exist, if we can see them, within the treadmill. The saga teaches men to see and honor the humanness of the natural virtues, such as courage, patience, endurance, self-sacrifice, and the like. Among numerous examples, a classic instance of the saga, or epic, is Homer's *Odyssey*, the story of Ulysses and his wanderings in antiquity.

As we read or hear the great sagas, whether of ancient or of modern time, we may be moved by the desire to embody a kindred kind of heroism. Thus in Tennyson's *Ulysses* we can sense the impression created by Homer's *Odyssey* on a modern mind, as expressed in Tennyson's familiar words:

> Come, my friends,
> 'Tis not too late to seek a newer world.
> Push off, and sitting well in order
>   smite
> The sounding furrows; for my purpose holds
> To sail beyond the sunset, and the
>   baths
> Of all the western stars, until I die.

The saga at its best has a two-fold value: it shows wherein the nobility of great character lies and it shows the heroism of the common life. Even when trivial and preposterous, it still serves to lift the hearer a little way above the treadmill. But by its nature it is *humanism* in poetry or symbol. It sings, but its notes are essentially bound by the human horizon. Its theme is that of Virgil in the famous opening line of the *Aeneid:*

> *Arma virumque cano*
> (I sing of arms and of the man)

If there is more than that in the sum of things to be sung, the saga cannot sing it.

In saying this it is not forgotten that the saga may teem with gods; indeed, the *Odyssey*, here used as the classic example, is a case in point. But just the same the saga is secular in the root meaning of that term; that is, it concerns the people and the events of a *saeculum*, a particular age or generation; and again we must say that if there is more to sing than the *saeculum* in which the saga is laid, the saga cannot sing it.

THE PILGRIMAGE

In the third of the views with which we are here concerned, life is a pilgrimage. Observe where the great differences lie between life as treadmill, as saga, and as pilgrimage.

The name of pilgrim has ordinarily been given to men and women who have escaped from some unbearable treadmill and have gone out on a journey both of mind and of body in quest of some shrine, as was so commonly done during the Middle Ages; or in quest of a land where they hoped to construct a society embodying their religious and political ideals. The pilgrim in this sense has, of course, played an incalculably great part in laying American foundations, not only in settling the Bay Colony, but also in opening up our Western States as well.

But pilgrimage is a state of mind before it is a journey, and many who deserve to be known as pilgrims can never take a journey of body. Yet they refuse to live in a treadmill. For some, who are pilgrims at heart, have to spend their days in the same round of constantly repeated activities as their fellows; but to them it is no longer a treadmill. For them, as for Jacob while he was serving his seven years for Rachel, the flow of psychological time has been speeded up by a new motive and the sense of monotony has no place in their living.

The differences between life as pilgrimage and life as saga are equally great. Life as saga, we saw, is life bounded in two planes. It can celebrate humanity, but it is essentially limited *to* humanity. And it can celebrate the *saeculum*, the current time, but it is limited *to* time.

Life as pilgrimage, on the contrary, is open in both of the planes where life as saga is closed. In the vertical plane, so to speak, where life as saga is closed, life as pilgrimage is open to more than the merely natural and human, so that human existence is consciously related not only to nature and to humanity, but *also to God who transcends nature and humanity*. And in the horizontal plane, if we may again use a spatial symbol, where life as saga is secular in the sense of being limited by time, life as pilgrimage is open to eternity. It tastes what has been strikingly called "the power of an endless life." [1]

We have now to inquire how one may pass back and forth between life as treadmill or saga, and life as pilgrimage; and in particular we shall wish to ask what part is played in this passage by the crises of experience.

LIFE IN THE BIBLICAL VIEW

At birth a new human being emerges, and we say that this new creature has life. If pressed to say what "life" is, we are soon overwhelmed with difficulties. But when we speak of human life, we ordinarily imply at least two things: that there is a body, and that there is a soul, or psyche.

Philosophy is divided as to the nature of the relation between body and soul. Philosophers with a Platonic bent tend to regard the two as distinct. Those whose training is in the sciences, however, are more likely to regard body and psyche as a unity, and this view gains weight with the development of a modern branch of medicine known as "psychosomatic medicine," in which the intimate relation between *psyche* and *soma* (body) in the production and healing of "physical" as well as "mental" illness, is the subject of study and the ground of therapy.

In the Biblical view of man body and soul are commonly regarded as a unity. In that view the soul or psyche is not a separate entity which has come to take up residence in a body; rather, the psyche is life itself, the life principle which animates the body. Thus body and soul together constitute so close a unity that a modern reader will have much difficulty in following Biblical thought unless he is prepared to recognize that to a Biblical writer, both consciousness and the emotions are seated through the whole body, not only in the intellect, but also in the heart, the diaphragm, the kidneys, the bowels, and so on. The soul or psyche is the life which animates the whole, and is breathed into man by God.[2]

Furthermore, in the Biblical view this body-soul is of the order of nature. That is to say, in the ancient Biblical view, and now in the modern scientific view, the soul or psyche exists in a plane with which we are all familiar, an "earthly" plane, which any who will, may examine and study. In fact the ancients were shrewd observers, and apt in their generalizations. Such books as Proverbs and Ecclesiastes contain much of this ancient lore, describing the devious ways of the psyche with an earthy realism which is so striking now, because so true in any age.

GROWTH

In animate nature there is an inward propulsion to grow. In plant life, for example, the seed when placed in suitable surroundings, will germinate, swell, send out roots, send up a sprout, break into leaf, and eventually complete its cycle by producing seed again after its kind. This it does as if by a sort of inner compulsion. So strong is this compulsion that, in growing, a tree, for example, will lift, push, or split heavy obstructing objects in order to complete itself.

In animal life a similar phenomenon is to be seen. A young bird, for instance, acts as if there were an inner compulsion to learn to fly, to leave the nest, to sing, to mate, to feed and defend its own young, to migrate, and so on.

And in the human being we have also to reckon with a comparable kind of inward propulsion to grow, that is, *to pass through certain stages as one moves toward the complete fulfilment of life.* Some of these stages of growth and the inward propulsion to pass into them are very obvious, for they involve the body, and only very rarely does an individual fail to emerge from the womb, and, if living, to increase in size, weight, and height; to walk, to talk, to become pubescent, and so on.

In the case of the psyche or soul there are stages, too, as truly as for the body. To specify these with any sense of completeness in the analysis is a baffling task, for human psychic development is highly complicated. With reasonable confidence, however, we may speak of five great stages,[3] and of a deep inner propulsion to achieve them. They are:

1. Becoming an individual, a stage typical of childhood.
2. Becoming weaned away from the parents; typical of adolescence.
3. Finding one's basic identifications, typical of young maturity.
4. Achieving a mature view of life and the universe; this may be achieved early, but it is a typical quest of middle life.
5. Achieving simplification of life in its physical, material and spiritual aspects so that the soul may with less and less impediment progress toward its chosen destiny; typical of old age.

Now the inward propulsion to achieve these stages, or some such stages as these, is very strong. It is a powerful thrust from within, keeping infant and child in restless activity of body and psyche. It keeps the adolescent in tension with his personal environment. It drives the young to seek the niche they will fill in social and economic life. It keeps those of more mature years feeling empty still until they have gained some satisfying sense of at-homeness in the total universe of thought and affairs. And as he nears the horizon of life as he has known it thus far, it impels him to set his inward house in order for whatever he believes still awaits him beyond the veils of time and sense.

From the angle of psychology we can say that this inward propulsion is of the order of nature, for it is instinctual, not learned. Those who prefer the language of psychology may see in it, if they choose, a manifestation of what has been called "the life instinct."

From the angle of Biblical thought we can say that it has been given us by God, and it is good, very good. It may well be that this is some part of what is meant when it is said that man was made in the image of God.

SHRINKING BACK

If this were all there is to the story of the human psyche, there would be little to human history except the recounting of the idyllic tale of happiness and progress. But the psyche knows another motive, one which seems to be peculiar to the human being, apparently not being found either in plant or animal life. It runs exactly counter to the inward propulsion to growth. It is a dread and fear of growth, a shrinking back from the hardships, the risks and dangers, the suffering, which are involved in each stage of growth.

It is to be found in some form at every potential stage of growth. The infant emerges from the physical womb, but the psyche can decide only after prolonged struggle whether to emerge from the psychic womb of safety, or to stay enmeshed within it. The youth wishes to shake himself free of his parents, yet as the years roll on child and parent may find themselves locked together by imprisoning bonds which neither is capable of breaking. In young maturity one who has achieved a certain type of free individuality, may miss the deeper fulfilments of young maturity because he is afraid of the mature responsibilities of marriage, parenthood, parental love, business, state and religion. Toward middle life, one may find his philosophy of life wholly inadequate to the demands placed upon it, and yet from pride or fear he may shrink from the frightening task of reorienting life. And as old age approaches, one may refuse to face it, clinging desperately to the outward trappings of youth, reckoning his golden age as somewhere in the past, and thus in his boastful refusal to grow old he is already dying, but does not know it.

In all these and a thousand more like them, the soul takes on the role of Lot's wife. Looking backward to the good things about to be left behind, and unable to go forward, one is immobilized into a pillar of salt which cannot escape from its own desolation.

If one wishes a psychological term for this shrinking back, it is at least partly akin to what has been called the death instinct.

From the angle of religious thought, shrinking back comes as a result of temptation, or "testing." And in Biblical language it is written of the Son of Man that His temptations to draw back from the hard way were of Satan. That is to say, the motive of shrinking back is, in the speech of some modern theologians, demonic. In the last analysis this, as much as many other things of which the term is used, is rebellion against God.

CRISES

At any time, from infancy to old age, crises may arise in the individual life. In any one of a myriad combinations of outward and inward events, one finds himself in circumstances where he feels the propulsion to pass over some sort of Jordan and enter upon some new level of responsibility and recompense. And yet this new step forward is a step into the unknown, peopled with dangerous creatures of fact, as truly as with menacing creations of fancy. The stage one has already reached in growth is good, though not yet fully satisfying. In that case is it better to bear the ills we know, or fly to others that we know not of? So the motive of growth is met by the motive of shrinking back. In that time of conflict, we have come to crisis, whether we are one year old, or three score years and ten.

Now crisis can be conceived and dealt with in purely secular terms, if we so choose. That is, crisis can be regarded as occurring, as indeed it does, in the present moment of our *saeculum,* the precise temporal hour in which we happen to be living. In that event if a crisis proves unmanageable within the limits of the person's resources, the person may seek to solve the crisis by some drastic means such as violence to himself or others, or he may seek help from some qualified source such as psychologist or psychiatrist.

It is not enough to say merely that such help is competent, assuming now that this is so; it needs to be seen also that such assistance may draw upon insights not commonly possessed by any other persons at present available in society. There is not the slightest intention of discounting its value when we say what must now also be said, namely, that when a crisis is met at the secular plane, the solution, too, will have to remain in the secular plane, at least as far as conscious apprehension of the meaning of the solution is concerned. It is a solution at the level of the saga. That solution may succeed in bringing the person out of the treadmill and into his own saga. That in itself is good, a thing to be sung. But if a pilgrim aspect of the crisis is possible, or even conceivable, the secular solution by its own nature is incapable of entering that cosmic realm.

But crisis can also be conceived and dealt with in religious terms. In that case the very same events can be given, not merely a temporal setting, but also a setting which is universal and eternal. And the solution of crisis, in this case, becomes a happening which transpires in the order of nature, but in its deeper essence it is seen to be of the order of grace, emerging for the benefit of man from a source which is beyond man.

There are religious terms to express this wider, universal and eternal significance which is latent in every human crisis. Three of the more notable of these are confrontation, judgment, and faith.   Let us examine the meaning of these terms as they bear upon crisis.

CONFRONTATION

By "confrontation" is simply meant that in crisis, God confronts man. That is to say, the crisis, which is a time of decision as between advancing into growth or shrinking back from its perils, is a time when God confronts the human creature.

The literature of the Jewish-Christian heritage abounds in illustrations of this type of experience. These instances have one common thread running through them all, which is this: the individual, facing some crisis in which he was being torn loose from the comfortable moorings where he had arrested himself, apprehends it also as a fact of experience that his crisis was not of purely personal concern to himself alone; God was present in the combination of circumstances which were placed before him. They vary, however, in the degree to which the recognition of God as confronting man is on the instant during the crisis, or later in retrospect.

Note a few typical instances in which the recognition is at the very hour of confrontation, and at the same time observe how wide is the variety in the circumstances which make up the crisis itself. For example, there is Abraham, having already left Ur with its high state of culture, and dwelling now with his clan in Haran, comfortable enough in his new life there; yet confronted by the demand to leave all this and his father's clan as well, to go on a still greater journey from which there could be no turning back.[4] Or Jacob; having deceived his father and brought down on himself the fury of his brother, is running away from the damage which he has wrought; he reaches Bethel, lies down to sleep, dreams, and awakes with the shuddering recognition, "Surely the Lord is in this place, and I knew it not." [5]

Again, there is Isaiah, the young aristocrat; evidently he had identified himself deeply with Uzziah, a king whose power and prestige were great. When Uzziah died, it must have seemed to Isaiah that all the supports of life had given way. But then, "In the year that King Uzziah died, I saw also the Lord high and lifted up." [6] Or there is Ezekiel, whose dearly loved wife is referred to as "the desire of thine eyes." But there came a day when he knew that she was to be taken from him by death; and that was a day when he heard "the voice of the Lord," bringing him understanding of the way he could transcend the bereavement.[7]

Or there is Paul, fighting desperately to maintain status and self-respect within the limits of his childhood's religion, venting his hostility under the sanction of his religion; he is confronted while on the very errands of his faith by the risen Christ, with revolutionizing effect.[8] And so it goes, with no end to the instances; Manoah and his wife, a childless couple, who are apprised that they are to have a child, and who must then reorient all their living;[9] Peter, disillusioned in the outcome of his hopes for his countrymen, going back to his fishing; the Emmaus-bound friends, stalled in their discussions of religion—all suddenly know themselves confronted by Deity.

Nor does the story end with the Biblical accounts. On the contrary, it could be traced century by century to our own day as one figure after another in a great succession has found himself, in some crisis, confronted by the bidding to go beyond what he then was, in order that he might approach a little nearer to what he might be; and in being so confronted has known, each after his own manner of describing it, that he had come face to face with God.

And there is also the case of those whose confrontation has been more slowly recognized for what it was, and who have expressed the meaning in the more formal language about God which we call theology. For instance, Joseph, looking back over the course of a tumultuous life, seeing how often he had been shaken out of his comfortable security, could say, "Ye thought evil against me, but God meant it unto good."[10] God meant it! So with those notable figures who, looking through their own total experience of confrontation, have shaped the classic language of theology; such figures as Paul, Augustine, Francis of Assisi, Brother Lawrence, Luther, Calvin, Wesley, John Bunyan, Jonathan Edwards, Kierkegaard, Karl Barth—the list would have no end.

But in order to realize the strength of this heritage, we need to go beyond the great household names so familiar in Christian thought, and include also the unknown figures; the housewives, the teachers, the farmers, the clerks, the laborers, in short, the ordinary people of all time who have known every hardship and tragedy but who, as spiritual life ripens and mellows, look back over the whole and are profoundly convinced that "He led me all the way."

JUDGMENT

The time of crisis and of confrontation is also a time of judgment. Indeed, in the Greek language, in which the New Testament is written, the word "crisis" *means* "judgment." That is, in the hours of crisis the soul is under divine judgment.

In principle, three ways are open in periods of crisis: to go forward beyond the stage which one has already reached; or to stay where one is; or to retreat to a still earlier and lower stage. Both the second and the third of these, staying or retreating, are a shrinking back. And in a most expressive passage in the Epistle to the Hebrews, the divine appraisal is put in these words: "If he shrink back, my soul hath no pleasure in him." [11]

What is this but to say that such a one, by shrinking back, cuts himself off from the constructive, healing, redeeming, strengthening, and joy-giving power resident in the universe? Cut off from these, he is exposed the more surely to the consequences which must inevitably follow upon the violation of the very principles upon which the universe itself is laid down. If strong, such a one may lay about him titanically, like some Samson or Hitler, until he has pulled down the pillars of temple or nation about him, sweeping others with him down into ruin and utter chaos. If he is of feebler stripe he may approach with every crisis a little nearer to being a zero, inert in the social order, or a parasite whom others must support, or an invalid.

It requires no crashing heavens to display the judgment of God. His judgments are within us, and lying as open sores all about us for any who can read to see.

In religious thought shrinking back is called by many terms, but the classic term for this attitude is unbelief.

FAITH

Conversely, the religious term for the contrasted attitude is *faith*. The two attitudes of unbelief and of faith, with their consequences, are clearly set out in two passages from Hebrews; for that Epistle, in one manner of viewing it, is a treatise on faith and unbelief.

And to whom sware he [God] that they should not enter into his rest, but to them that were disobedient? And we see that they were not able to enter in because of unbelief.[12]

For yet a very little while, he that cometh shall come, and shall not tarry; but my righteous one shall live by faith: and if he shrink back, my soul hath no pleasure in him.

But we are not of them that shrink back unto perdition, but of them that have faith to the saving of the soul.[13]

And now, with this view of faith before us, let us return for a moment to the thought of life as treadmill, as saga, and as pilgrimage. There we saw that life as treadmill and as saga is life conceived as being restricted to the plane of the human and the secular.

But the attitude which views life as a pilgrimage and raises it above both treadmill and saga, is precisely the attitude to which the writer of the Epistle to the Hebrews gives the name of *faith*. In his famous defining sentence he observes that "faith is the substance of things hoped for, the evidence of things not seen." [14] In order to appreciate the boldness of his statement, one needs to follow the argument in the preceding chapters of his Epistle.

The thread of that argument as far as it concerns us here is of this nature. There are two orders of existence. One of these is the earthly; it is what we now commonly call history. Its two great characteristics are, first, that it is temporal and therefore will eventually come to an end; the other, that it is not completely subject to God. The second order of existence he calls "the heavens," or the "heavenly." This refers to what we now commonly call the cosmic or the universal. But it has two great characteristics which we do not always attribute to those terms; namely, it is eternal, and it is completely subject to God. These two characteristics of the "heavenly" or cosmic order are of primary importance if we would follow the thought.

Furthermore, according to the writer of this Epistle, in "the heavens," that is in the cosmic or eternal order, there are certain forms of reality which may be called archetypes. Although the archetypes are eternal, they can be known and experienced during the earthly and temporal existence in either of two ways.

One way in which an archetype can be known is by means of its pattern, or its shadow, or its figure. For an eternal archetype can have a pattern, or copy, on earth.[15] Or the archetype may, as it were, cast a shadow on earth, a shadow which partly reveals the nature of the archetype.[16] Or the archetype may be partly known by means of a "figure," or similitude which shows some likeness to the archetype.[17] Of these three terms the strongest is the "pattern," for it corresponds to what we mean nowadays when we refer to one specimen of an entire species; when we know a specimen, we know a true part of a species, although we do not know the entire species. But all three, the pattern, the shadow, and the figure, yield a true, although only a partial, knowledge of the archetype.

The other way in which the archetype can be known is by means of the "substance" or the "image" of the archetype.[18] "Substance" we may think of as the archetype itself, going out from the eternal order into the temporal order of history,[19] and it is exactly as real as God Himself is real, since God is spoken of as a "substance."[20] And we may think of the "image" (*charakter*) as being an exact reproduction of the archetype.[21] The "substance," to repeat, is the very archetype itself which has gone forth from the cosmic and eternal order into the earthly and temporal order of history.

To recapitulate: According to this Epistle, eternal reality may be both revealed *to* man and known *by* man, in any one of five modes. They are the following; beginning with the least clear and complete, and moving toward the most clear and complete:

1. The figure (*parabole*); a likeness, drawn from another realm.
2. The shadow (*skia*); a reflection cast by the thing itself.
3. The pattern (*hypodeigma*); a copy, a specimen of a species.
4. The image (*charakter*); an exact reproduction.
5. The substance (*hypostasis*); the archetype itself, i.e., the eternal reality itself going forth into the temporal order.

Among the principal archetypes in the eternal order which are set forth in this Epistle, three stand out as of the utmost significance. They are: first, God Himself; second, the remission of sins; and third, eternal life. Of these three, the Old Testament gave man the pattern, or the shadow, or the figure; while "the new and living way" which is recorded in the New Testament gave men either the image, or else the very substance itself. As for God, Jesus Christ is His "image" or *charakter*.[22] The sacrifice of himself which Jesus Christ made is the substance of eternal redemption.[23] And then comes the daring leap of thought which places the benefits of all this at our very door to have if we will: *faith is the actual substance of eternal life, enjoyed here and now within the temporal order of history, giving pragmatic evidence of things as yet not seen by mortal eyes.*[24]

What faith does for man while he still lives in the temporal order of history is illustrated with abundant detail in the eleventh chapter of this Epistle. Faith is, so to say, the organ or instrument by which man, while still living in time and enmeshed still in nature and in history, may yet pass really and actually into the eternal order of existence. He has the substance, that is, the actuality, of the things hoped for, and has them now, in danger, in suffering, in defeat or in victory, in the years of long-delayed fruition as truly as in the hours of ecstatic fulfilment. His is the life of the pilgrim who, while seeking the better country, has already begun to find it and live within it. His life is now open in its two dimensions: it is open to God as revealed in Jesus Christ who is the "image" of God; and it is open to eternity through faith which is the "substance," or actuality, of an order of life which is above time and nature.

THE SPIRIT

In Biblical thought this new life can be regarded from either of two points of view. When seen from the human side it is a life of faith. When seen from the divine side it is a life of the Spirit.

For in the Biblical view, God takes the initiative in confronting man. At a particular point in history there was a supreme and unique confrontation by means of the person, Jesus Christ. That confrontation is prolonged in history by means of the Personal Spirit, variously called by such terms as the Spirit of Christ, the Spirit of God, the Holy Spirit, or simply the Spirit. The Spirit prolongs the unique confrontation which befell men in a bodily form.

Man's response, as we have just said, is faith. The result is new life, a "new creation." This newness of life is often regarded as a decisive transformation, so radical as to mark the beginnings of a new life which had not before existed. In John it is called being "born anew" (or "from above").[25] Paul is fond of the term "resurrection" to indicate an even more radical transformation which can be expressed only by the symbol of being raised from the dead, here and now, to a new life which is a life of the Spirit.

This new life can be viewed as "a life of the Spirit" both because it is a creative act of the Spirit of God, and because it is indwelt by that same Spirit. It is not entirely clear whether Paul thinks of the human being as having a dormant spirit which is awakened, as it were, from death to become a living spirit under the activity of the divine Spirit; or whether he thinks of human "spirit" as never existing at all in a given person until implanted or breathed in by the divine Spirit. Such conceptions as rebirth and resurrection, both referring to present life, perhaps give weight to the first of these possibilities, that is, the dormant human spirit called to life by the divine Spirit.

But in any event human spirit, whether quickened from dormancy, or called out of non-being into being, or brought about by a wholly new creative act, is different from *soul;* and it would appear that, strictly speaking, soul or psyche on the one hand, and spirit on the other, cannot be taken as synonyms. Soul, as we have repeatedly remarked, is of the order of nature, while man's spirit is of a spiritual order; that is, it is of the divine and eternal order of existence.

So, to say it once again for emphasis, if new life results from God's confrontation of man, this new life can be called a life of the spirit, because man's spirit has now been brought to life; or it can be called a life of the Spirit, because of the creative initiative of the divine Spirit; or yet again it can be called a life of faith, because of man's response to the divine initiative.

And this new life of the Spirit is a life which is *constantly* being confronted by God, repeatedly, over and over, on and on as the years go by. In New Testament writings this activity of God in the believer's life is ordinarily expressed in terms of the Holy Spirit, who is now within man in the new life of the Spirit. As indwelling Spirit, he is shown, on the one hand, as bringing assurance of acceptance by God, with resulting peace which is greater than mere intellectual understanding, and with joy which arises continually in any surroundings like pure water springing forth from unpolluted depths.

And yet, on the other hand, the Spirit is shown as constantly confronting man both inwardly and outwardly, with promptings and with disturbances of any complacent spiritual *status quo.* The outward confrontation is especially to be seen in "the means of grace," particularly in the Word of God and in the sacraments, which are outwardly given but to be inwardly appropriated, thus giving rise in turn again both to inward assurance and to promptings. The result is commonly spoken of as "sanctification," which is not perfection now achieved, but rather is a growth toward that state.

NOT PEACE, BUT A SWORD

If one has followed the thought thus far he is now asked to go one step further and recognize that the function of religion in the Jewish-Christian stream is not merely to bring peace and comfort; its function, just as truly, is to disturb us repeatedly within the very peace and comfort which we enjoy. If its function were *only* to bring peace and comfort, religion would basically be a denial of life, for life does not so serve us. But rather, and contrary to much that is commonly assumed, Christianity embodies the profoundest possible *acceptance* of life, in the sense that it discloses a way to deal with the peace-disturbing aspects of existence and transmute them into good. Thus we have the paradox that the soul can be made perfect only through suffering.

The classic expression concerning this role of the Christian religion is the saying of Jesus: "Think not that I am come to send peace on the earth: I came not to send peace, but a sword." [26]

For it is precisely when man is *in* peace, comfort, security, satisfaction and complacency that God confronts him in crisis and in judgment.

It now remains to give more direct statement to three points which have already been suggested. One is that the garments which God wears, so to speak, when confronting man very often are no other than the circumstances which confront a man and which require of him a decision to grow, or to stay as he is, or to regress. It is these circumstances which compel us to decide, and these circumstances of the common life may be the form in which God comes again into our little part of human history, coming thus to our senses, confronting us, calling on us for the response of faith to the end that we may "enter in" a little further.

Again, these crises and these confrontations are not restricted to any one age or period of life. They begin in infancy, and they do not end short of the final hour of physical life.

And before we begin to consider the various stages in particular, another point is to be stressed as applying generally to them all. It may be called the foundational aspects of growth. For each stage, when we live through it in such a way as to meet adequately the demands it lays on us, leaves behind, as it were, a deposit of growth; it becomes an asset and a resource for each succeeding stage. On the other hand, each stage where we fail to meet adequately the demands it lays upon us, leaves behind it a deposit of the very opposite kind, a defect, or perhaps a weak or even malignant spot in the foundations of life. And this weak or malignant place in the foundation has a way of acting constantly afterward as a barrier or a plague-source to keep us from the completeness which we might otherwise attain.

These points we shall seek to elaborate more fully in the chapters that are to follow as we take up various stages in the life which is being confronted at each stage by the call to go on toward completeness.

CHAPTER TWO

A Child Is Born

WE ARE NOW to begin in thought with an infant who is newly born into the world, and about to start his journey in it. From the moment of his birth, hundreds of practical questions arise. But these must not divert us from the central fact that an infant is not born into a vacuum, but rather into a living world of living people. We shall miss the most important insights at the very outset if we assume that he can be weighed, fed, measured, tested, and "trained" as if he were in isolation.

The heading of this chapter, "A Child Is Born," is taken from an ancient book; but this clause, torn from its context, is misleading, just as misleading as it would be to try to consider a child torn from his social context. The full sentence from which the chapter heading is taken reads: "For *unto us* a child is born." [1] That is the true order, whether we look at the event of birth from the angle of biology, or of psychology, or of religion. For there must be a "we" before there can be an "I"; and again this is as true in religion as it is in psychology. Therefore in this chapter, although we begin with the newborn infant, we must also begin with the parents.

CHILDHOOD

In order to simplify this highly complex period in the life of an individual, we may liken childhood to a drama lasting, say, some eleven years. This drama has its principal characters, its various acts, and its central problem for each character.

The principal characters in the drama are the infant, his mother, and his father. There may, of course, be other principal characters who are present and felt in the drama, such as other children, older or younger; grandparents, aunts, uncles, and so on. The possible combinations are very numerous. But the key persons for our purposes still are the three—infant, mother, and father. If one wishes to think of an eternal triangle in the drama of life, this is it.

The drama has three long acts. The first, infancy, we may regard as lasting for some three years. The second is early childhood, lasting, say, from three until about six years of age. The third is middle and later childhood, from about six through perhaps the tenth or eleventh year. It need hardly be said that ages can be stated only in the most general approximations. The central problem for the child, as he lives through the struggles of this drama, is called individuation. The problem of individuation can be stated in its *simplest* terms in either of two ways. From the child's point of view the question is, "How can I become an individual?"—although obviously he does not express the struggle in such words as those. From the point of view of the parents or the observer the question is, "What kind of individual will this child become, in the setting in which he lives these first years?"

As we shall see in greater detail through the rest of the chapter the central problem of childhood, namely individuation, is not presented to a child all at once, nor can it be solved all at once. Rather, in actual life it is broken down into a series of more specific problems of growth. Under favorable conditions these more specific problems of growth can be solved one at a time as they arise. Thus in infancy the infant faces his first and earliest problems of growth; in early childhood the problem of growth is broadened and takes on a somewhat different form; and similarly again in the third act of middle and later childhood. And furthermore, the solution which is found in infancy becomes the basis for the kind of solution which can be achieved in early childhood; and that, in turn, affects the kind of solution which is possible in middle and later childhood.

PARENTAL ADEQUACY

The kind of individuation which the child can achieve is governed to a large degree by what may be called parental adequacy.

In part this parental adequacy depends on the solutions of the problems of growth which the mother and the father in their turn were able to achieve up to the time of their marriage. The mother and the father each brought to the marriage what they had become up to the day of the marriage. For both the mother and the father had earlier passed, each of them, through his own drama, not only of childhood, but also of youth as well. They bring to the marriage their own two characters, each as it had developed in *their* parental homes and wherever else either of them may have lived.

And in further part the parental adequacy depends on the nature of the interaction between these two characters, the mother and the father, after the marriage.

Thus the infant is, as it were, born into the confluence of two great and long streams of character, streams which have flowed down from the remote past into today, streams which have now flowed together in marriage. And now this new joint stream awaits the infant, takes him into its own embrace, and carries him forward into his own future.

And just as the child now faces his own problem of individuation even as his parents before him faced theirs, so too the parents now, with such adequacy as they have achieved before and after their marriage, begin to face their own fresh, new issues in *their* growth as lovers and as parents. More than that, just as their child does not face his problem of individuation all at once, so the mother and the father as wife and husband do not face their own issues of growth all at once, but rather face them in a new form at each stage of the child's growth. So for all the persons of the drama, infant, mother, and father, the drama is not only infinitely varied, but is also, as it were, on a moving stage where each year, or better let us say each day, confronts all of them with fresh growth demands.

In this chapter we shall be obliged to give a certain amount of attention to parental adequacy, since this so deeply affects the child's individuation. But for the most part we shall wait until Chapter IV to give larger consideration to the demands upon their own growth which the parents encounter as their children are born and strive to grow. For the present we turn again to the infant, and the various stages of his drama, that drama which is as old as the race of man, yet as new as the last infant born into the world.

INFANCY

The infant emerges into what, to him, is an undifferentiated mass of being. Helpless and utterly dependent, he of course knows nothing of "mother," "father," or aught else. But we for our part, thinking of his situation, must look ahead and be reminded of what he naturally cannot yet know; and that is that he has entered a world in which he has already encountered, and afterward will always be encountering, two great classes of being. He must establish some kind of relation with each of these two classes of being. This is his first great confrontation, coming to him both from nature and from God. And it is of the utmost significance that the kind of relation he will sustain to each, begins to be established from the very hour of his birth.

One of these classes of being is *persons*. On the instant of his birth he is confronted by persons. Even in the extreme case of the unattended birth he encounters the mother, not now as a part of her but as separated from her, yet needing her. At the hour of his birth he encounters persons, or at least and inevitably one person; and thenceforth and until the hour of his physical death he will be surrounded by persons. If his life proves even remotely to approach what we think of as normal, he will literally be surrounded by persons, more or fewer in number, until breath ceases. And, on the other hand, should it later develop that he hates all persons, turns against them all, and strives by some means to flee from all persons by completely withdrawing into himself or by fleeing to some desert or island to be alone, even so the basic formula of his life will still be shaped, though negatively, around persons.

His primary character need is that of learning to relate to persons. And in infancy, which is the first act of his drama, he makes his first beginnings in the vast sea of human relationships, by means of his relation with the person closest to him and on whom he is most dependent for affection, food, comfort, and security. That person ordinarily is his mother.

The other order of being which confronts the infant is *things*. Things surround him at the instant of birth; and as with persons, so too with things—even more inexorably than in the case of persons—things will continue to surround him with no moment of exception until he has ceased to breathe, and even then things will receive his body into their still embrace. Food, toys, clothing, bed and other articles of furniture; house, money, car, books, works of art; all nature, animate and inanimate; countryside, village, or city; banks, bonds, stores piled with "goods," factories, weapons, armaments; things by day and by night; things at hand and things in the sky out to unimaginable distances; things shifting in value and interest as he grows, but things at every age of his life—he is incessantly surrounded by things.

And if his primary character need is that of learning to relate to persons, his second character need is that of learning to relate to things. And in infancy he makes his first beginnings of relating to this other vast sea of being, that of things. And as we shall see,

the way in which he begins to meet this second character need in
infancy will be deeply influenced by the way in which his primary
character need begins to be met.

The way in which the child's primary character need begins to
be met, that is, the kind of relation to persons which the infant
begins to have, is profoundly influenced and perhaps determined,
by parental adequacy. We have already tried to indicate what is
meant by that term. But let us put it again by saying that basically
we now mean a deep emotional readiness for this child before he
is born, and an equally deep emotional acceptance of him after he
is born, and as he grows.

This emotional readiness, or any lack of it or any substitute for
it, will come to the child first ordinarily from the mother, and will
first be felt by him in his relation with the mother in the daily
events and routine, such as holding, feeding, tone of voice, bath-
ing, toilet training, and so on, through the thousand of early contacts where *feeling* in the mother calls forth the appropriate an-
swering feeling in the infant. All this of course is long before the
infant can utter his first word.

But the mother's adequacy, in its turn, is profoundly influenced
by two factors: the way she herself lived through her own drama
as child and youth; and the quality of the emotional relationship
now existing between herself and her husband. In other words,
both husband and wife are equally, although differently, involved
in parental adequacy. Under favorable conditions each is able to
supply the other's emotional needs, and in consequence it is as if
there were an illimitable supply of genuine and outgoing love to
sustain each other and the infant, and to begin to draw forth from
the infant his own responding feeling of the same kind.

But as with the wife, so too with the husband: his own earlier
drama of childhood and youth has deeply influenced his own emotional adequacy, first for marriage and then for parenthood. And
to this is now added the nature of the relationship with the wife.
If he is unable through his own inadequacy to supply the wife's

normal emotional needs, an abnormal emotional drain is taken out
of the mother in her relation with the infant, and this drain on
her may prove greater than her capacity unreplenished by the
husband, can supply.

Or if the wife's own adequacy is limited because of her own
abnormal need for attention and affection, the husband's adequacy, supposing now that it is "normal," may prove insufficient
for the abnormal drain placed upon it. In either event the wife's
emotional needs cannot be kept replenished from their normal
source in the husband; and it is probable that she will turn elsewhere for emotional replenishment, seeking to supply the need
from the source most consonant with her own character development, such as the infant, or her own mother or father, or a lover,
and so on.

And now let us look at the results of this first act of the drama,
both as concerns the parents, and as concerns the infant. The results in each case may on the whole be favorable and constructive;
or they may be otherwise.

In the case of the parents, when the result is generally favorable
both the mother and the father show themselves capable of accepting and assuming the first responsibilities of parenthood. They can
accept the pregnancy as a fulfilment of love and as promising to
open yet another stage in their own fulfilment of life. They can
accept the infant, whichever the sex, as boy or girl; they can accept him, whatever his physique, appearance, and native endow-
ment; whatever the spacing in reference to their other children;
and whatever the economic situation which happens just then to
prevail in the household. They are able to give a genuine, outgoing,
uninterrupted love to each other and to the child *now*, and so
are better enabled also to pass without serious hampering into the
ensuing stages of the infant's growth; and they are also the better
able to pass with increasing adequacy into being parents of yet
other children, if others there should be.

But, on the other hand, man and wife who are not emotionally mature enough for parenthood may find themselves swamped by the responsibilities and their own inadequacy. They may find their own hostility toward each other more deeply aroused than their love; leading to mutual recrimination over this pregnancy, and with mounting dread of the childbirth. The mother may find labor prolonged and extremely hard, and thus is further prepared to enter motherhood as a martyr. Both husband and wife may be frightened by the whole experience, and not least by the unmanageable feelings which stir in them toward each other and toward the infant. These feelings may be repressed, thus tending to increase their own sense of guilt.

Then, not being able to give genuine, outgoing, and uninterrupted love to each other and to the infant, two other consequences may begin to follow. One is that they seek blindly to find substitutes to give to each other and to the child, in place of the deeper love which they cannot give. Here, in principle, the resort is to *things*, instead of love; things begin to be given, received, and treasured in place of warm and genuine love at its deepest levels—such things especially as food, toys, money, and clothing, all far in excess of casual and ordinary needs. These things are regarded by giver and recipient as tokens of love; but when they are not genuine tokens but substitutes, there is an overwhelming need to give, and an insatiable greed to receive, neither of which can come to rest in accepted fulfilment.

The other consequence may be that the parents produce excellent reasons for voiding the normal responsibilities of parenthood, such as the child's daily care, participation in his education, or even his presence in the household. Maids, nurses, nurseries, tutors, highly specialized schools at a distance, and the like are felt to be a necessity. They are secured, perhaps at great sacrifice, or perhaps again with considerable ostentation, and are presented to the child, to each other, and to their friends as outward symbols of an inward grace which they cannot give.

And now what of the infant? Where the results are generally

favorable we see two great foundations beginning to be laid down as a basis on which all later life both in the natural and in the eternal order can be reared. One is that the infant, in learning to relate to the parents, has already begun to learn how to relate to persons on an emotional level so deep as to permit his own deepest needs to begin to be met from the very start of life. Quickly and simply said, this is; but its further consequences are beyond all imagining. This is the pearl of great price, but it cannot be bought with all a man's possessions and more. It can only be communicated by giving it, and it can only be possessed by accepting it and responding in kind.

The other consequence is that having encountered and received this genuine, outgoing and uninterrupted love from the beginning, he is not put under the necessity of finding substitutes for it in things. He can then make things be his servant, not his master. He can use things as means to chosen ends, and does not have to make things be ends in themselves. His primary security is in personal relations, not in things. Therefore, things can shift around him without causing the kind of panic likely to be felt by the person who is more basically related to things than to persons.

When parental adequacy is not sufficient for the demands thrown on it the results in the infant are, broadly speaking, of an opposite kind both as to persons and as to things. But the actual results of being deprived early of genuine, outgoing, uninterrupted love and of being presented with substitutes for it in early life, are so intricate, so farreaching, and so varied in nature and degree as to defy any brief statement. Here we can do no more than point briefly to a few characteristic *later* outcomes for which the foundations may be laid in infancy.

For example, it may become far more difficult and in some cases impossible for this person, first in infancy and then in later years, to relate easily and deeply to other persons as he encounters them. He seems to be on guard against getting close to others or letting them be close to him. He feels what is called ambivalence toward those few persons who are comparatively close to him; this double feeling of love and distrust, attraction and repulsion, seems to hold him back from entering into the deeper experiences of friendship and love. He wants to love, yet is afraid to love deeply, instinctively shrinking back; for he has been hurt so many times when he has tried to love that he dares not risk it again with the very person or persons whom he most longs to love.

Or he may show in a marked degree what is called "affect hunger," seeking hungrily for love and the proofs of love, yet never able to be satisfied; he seems to spend his life in avidly seeking more and yet more proofs of love which basically he is unable to believe in or accept in its profound simplicity and depth. He cannot secure the deeper love because he cannot give it; seeking from others what he himself is unable to give in return, he sucks up the life of others until they dread to see him approaching.

Or he may turn against others, more or less deeply. If he cannot give love, he *can* at least give hostility, in such ways as prolonged non-cooperation, or thwarting others, or producing severe behavior problems; and later it may be by pronounced aggressiveness, or delinquency, or criminality.

In such cases as affect hunger and turning against others, it may be seen that the person has been driven from a very early age to find a way in which he may deal with *suffering*. For the very young may suffer profoundly in their deprivation, the more so because they feel their situation as hopeless. So from very early years suffering may, as it were, be turned into a kind of capital to trade with. That is, it may be valued unconsciously, because it provides a way by which to bid for more of love's substitutes such as temporary attention, sympathy, and solicitude; or a fresh shower of things given; and so on. Or to display suffering and unhappiness may provide a way to punish those who have caused it, by causing them in turn to suffer also and thus perhaps bring them to remorse.

Or one who cannot give or receive genuine love may derive

another kind of satisfaction by dragging others into an abyss of misery like his own, that is, by causing others to suffer, especially in the case of those who are closest to him. It is as if he said, "Well, if I must writhe, you shall writhe all the more."

And in his relation to *things* the way is left the more open for two later developments which may provide a kind of external security to take the place of the deeper inner security which he has missed. One is the love of things. In this kind of development things take on a primary, not a secondary value; as in striving to possess things; obtaining them by any means, fair or foul, such as wheedling, trickery or stealing, or perhaps the more approved way of "the shrewd deal"; accumulating them, treasuring them, hoarding them. The "things" may be of any sort, from toys or old newspapers, to cars, hoards of cash or bonds, or what not.

The other result in relation to things is the compulsive necessity of having one's things at one's own complete private command. Thus, it may be, one must be able to do with his things exactly as he likes with no whit of outside interference. Or one must have his things in a certain place, or have them arranged in a precise order which must not be varied, or have them in exactly the right state of perfection; or he may use things in performing certain "rituals" which he feels impelled to enact in precisely the same way at the same time of the day or week. This compulsive necessity in dealing with things seems to be at least a part of the motivation of the meticulous person, or the perfectionist, or the compulsive character. This is the person who is thrown into panic or rage by the loss of things, or by a disturbance of his possession of them, or by a threat to his complete control of them, or by an upset of his routine in the use of them.

Then once more there is the case of the person who, from the outset of life, is not able to establish an outgoing relation of any kind either with persons or with things. Finding it impossible to relate to either of these two great classes of beings, either persons or things, only one world is left to him, and that is *himself*. Cut off both from persons and from things he may withdraw more or less completely into himself, drawing down the curtains ever more closely around himself. The world of persons being felt as a menace or an accusing threat, he may seal himself in with himself more and more tightly. Valuing things less and less, he may progressively lose interest in all things, even food.

This is the schizophrenic who, finding the world of persons *and* the world of things too much to cope with, shuts himself within himself. And then, finding that world a vacuum in no way replenished from without, there is nothing left but to die in complete isolation and disintegration. The absolute attitude of shrinking back has then taken its perfect toll.

EARLY CHILDHOOD

The second act of the drama of childhood is so complicated, as it unfolds day by day in actual life, that we cannot here follow it in its details. Nor is this the place to enter a discussion of the various interpretations of the essential nature of the struggle which goes on. Here it will be sufficient to say that a child is confronted not only by a world of persons and a world of things; but the world of persons which confronts him is a world of male and female.

The world of male and female comes to him from nature, for there it meets him at every turn. But there is more to the story than that, for it is a religious confrontation as well. This is nowhere better expressed than in the Genesis account of creation: [2] "Male and female created he them." For, "The Lord God said, it is not good that the man should be alone; I will make him an help meet for him. . . . And . . . the Lord God . . . made a woman and brought her to the man." Thenceforth woman confronts man, and man confronts woman. This is as much as to say that the fact of male and female is not merely a fact from nature; it is a fact from God.

It should be seen, too, that this is deeper than what is commonly called "sex." It would be better, with Hinsie, to refer to it as gender.[3] For there are the two great roles in life, of masculine and feminine; and these two not only confront, but hold the possibility of complementing and completing each other. In that sense, then, gender is more profound than sex, and the character problems it presents need to be solved at an earlier stage.

Now in the second act of the drama of childhood a child is placed in a situation where normally he must learn to relate to the parent of the opposite sex, as to male or to female as the case may be.

And it appears that the solution which is achieved will affect three further elements of character which grow out of, or are reared upon, the results of this second act. These are: first, the nature of the roles which the mother and the father, respectively, will have in the later life of the child as he advances in age; the kind of conscience the child will have; and the role which the child himself will take in life, as predominantly masculine or predominantly feminine.

As parents enter this period in a child's life, their adequacy is affected by all such factors as have already been considered. But now two other factors, already either latent or active in their characters, begin to be felt in fresh force in their relations with the child and in his response to them.

One is the extent to which they trust each other emotionally in their relations to the child. In the degree to which they trust each other deeply and completely in every phase of life, they can live farther into the drama of life as a whole and parenthood in particular, as partners who mutually support each other and take their respective roles as masculine and feminine in a way which supplies the two elements needed in every child's development. On the other hand, in the degree to which they cannot trust each other emotionally in their relations with the child, they become rivals for love from the child and the domination of him.

The other factor is the character of the parents themselves, as predominantly masculine or feminine. If the father is predominantly masculine and the mother predominantly feminine, then as far as these factors are concerned the parents are in a better position to meet the child's needs in this period. But if the mother is predominantly a masculine character, or the father predominantly a feminine character, then to that extent the child's need to relate both to a masculine man and a feminine woman are thrown out of balance.

The new tension in this period arises from the child's inner need to begin to be released from the infant's relation to the mother; for should he be unable to relax this earliest relationship with the mother and re-establish it on a more mature level, many kinds of growth which belong to later stages may prove impossible. The early initial release of the child *from* the mother is normally a release of the child *to* the father, that is, to a new and deeper relation of closeness to the father. But then, lest *this* relation be too close to permit growth, the father in turn is confronted by the need to release the child emotionally from too close a dependence upon *him;* and the child may enter a new closeness of relation with the mother on a basis which is not infantile. In principle this alternation of the greatest closeness of the child's relation with mother and father, respectively, may need to be repeated several times during childhood and adolescence, each time at a more advanced stage of maturity.

Where the results of this act of the drama are generally favorable, both the parents grow in the maturity of their love for each other and for the child. For each is able, as the need arises, to release the child from a closeness which is a necessity of growth, and yet becomes a prison if too prolonged. But where the drama cannot be lived through and instead is "frozen" at some intermediate point, either parent may begin subtly to dominate a son or daughter emotionally in a dominance-dependency relation from which the child can release himself later only after great suffering, if at all.

Where the results are generally favorable for the child, consider first the case of a boy. A boy in this case is able to relate on a deep, satisfying, and constructive basis with his father. This in turn is believed to affect the boy's growth of character in several important respects.

For one thing it appears to affect the nature of his conscience. The hostility which naturally arises in this as in all human relations need not be repressed, but can be handled in a relation where love is sound and strong; thus the deep sense of guilt which disturbs so many who have not successfully lived through this act is kept at a minimum, and the conscience can be of a more healthy kind.

Again, if a boy can identify deeply with his father, especially if the latter is predominantly masculine, the boy is that much the better equipped, himself, to take the masculine role in his own life.

And since such a boy is able to re-establish a close relation to his mother at a level beyond that of infancy, his attitude toward the mother, and toward other women later, can be of a more healthy kind than when he is kept in an infancy relation until he is adolescent or grown.

Where the results are less favorable the boy, being unable to secure release from the mother, may be unable to identify deeply with the father. Then in further consequence he may develop a morbid conscience, and find far greater difficulty in assuming a masculine role.

In the case of a girl, where the results are generally favorable, she is able to relate deeply to the father, but is able to relax that relation and relate again on a more mature level to the mother. This helps to break the closest infantile dependency on each, helps to create the basis for a wholesome conscience, and aids the girl in taking the feminine role in later life.

And conversely, where the girl cannot live through this act of the drama to a favorable outcome, she may remain too close to either the mother or the father, may prove to have a morbid conscience, and may be handicapped in taking up the feminine role as youth and woman.

MIDDLE AND LATER CHILDHOOD

In the third act of the drama of childhood the child begins to encounter the world of persons and things outside his family. Obviously his encounter with this world beyond the family does not
ordinarily wait until this time but now increasingly he begins to
enter the outer world for longer periods in the day and in situations where he is temporarily cut off from his family as in play
groups, school, church, and so on. It is as if the stage of his life
were expanding, with doors opening onto the stage on every side,
with people and yet more people pouring in around him.

Hence in this act of the drama his character need is to learn
to relate to persons outside the family. This need presents a child
with two demands: learning to relate to persons of about his own
age, especially to those of the same sex; and learning to relate to
persons who have, or who assume, some kind of authority over
him.

The results of the solutions found in the first two acts of the
drama begin to be more apparent as soon as the child goes out into
this enlarging stage.

Consider how true this is, first in the case of the child who has
been able to live through the earlier acts of the drama comparatively well. He is capable of relating to other persons with relative
ease and confidence. If he has been able to pass beyond an infancy
relation to his parents, boy is better able to encounter boy, and
girl to encounter girl, with a fair degree of assurance and without
morbid needs of boy for boy and girl for girl. We say of such a
child, "He gets on well with other children," or, "He has many
friends."

Such a child, having been able to relate well to his own parents,
is the more likely to relate well also to other persons in authority,
for if the persons in authority, as he encounters them, are capable
for their part of taking a friendly and not a bullying role, this child
can intuitively trust that person; such as teacher, policeman, guard,

and so on. This child then is likely to be able to pass into the life of boys or the life of girls, school life, and church life as a co-operative person, able "to take the gaff," able to conform to reasonable rules without resentment, presenting few serious behavior problems, and in no way a prig or a "sissy."

But if a child has come out of the earlier acts of his drama with still unsolved problems in his relations with either or both the parents he enters the third act handicapped for the wider human relations which now open to him.

Insecure basically, it is only natural that he should now experience fresh insecurity in relations with other children. The forms in which this insecurity may express itself are legion. He may be in more or less constant conflict with other children, as in snatching, taking their things, bullying, "picking on" them or hurting them. Or he may take up a morbid dependence, weaker boy on stronger boy, weaker girl on stronger girl. Or he may retreat from other children, shrinking away from play because it is "too rough," shrinking from participation with his group because they are "mean," "bad," or "nasty." He may become the prig who is better than his comrades, or the "sissy" who "can't take it" and stays at home.

Persons in authority are intuitively felt as a threat. Perhaps he requires an inordinate amount of attention from them, forever "running to teacher" or forever seeking the protection of the police, or, instead, he fights against authority, finding ways to outwit it, defying it, calling it down on his head, and in general setting himself against it with the greatest ingenuity. And he can do this whether it makes him a hero or an outcast in the eyes of his peers.

THE CONFRONTATION

Throughout the childhood of an individual there is a two-way confrontation constantly going on within a family. The parents en their side are confronted by the fact of the child and the demands for *their* growth which this living fact lays upon them. To this we shall return in Chapter IV. But the child, on his side, is confronted, as we have said, by his parents with such degree of adequacy and such view of life as they have achieved. Let us now examine this latter confrontation a little more closely, seeking to get at its meaning in terms of religion.

Many writings and discussions of religion in childhood appear to be based on two assumptions: first, that the teaching of religion begins at about the time a child is learning to talk; and second, that the content of that teaching is largely or entirely under the control of the person or persons who teach the child. One then proceeds, perhaps, to consider such points as the *words* in which the teaching shall be put, the *attitudes* to be cultivated, the *habits* to be developed, and so on. To express the matter in the baldest form it is as if we said, "Control what *goes in* by way of verbal teaching, then control what *comes out* by way of words and actions, and you have taught religion. So choose the time when you can commence to do this, determine what and how you wish to teach, and then *begin*." Put in this over-simple way, it is obvious that one is failing to reckon sufficiently with the *dynamic self of the child* which intervenes between the "teaching" and "the outcome."

But if we are to take due account of the dynamic self which intervenes between religion-presented and religion-responded-to, we must seek for the laws or principles which govern the way that dynamic self acts. The principle which governs the dynamic self in this respect can be stated, we believe, in some such way as this: *The emotional life of the individual as infant and child determines the kind of religion which he can respond to and make his own.*

The dynamic factors which confront the infant are the dynamic factors *outside* of him, and these begin to create the dynamic self *within* him. These dynamic factors ordinarily come to him first through his parents. We can recognize these dynamic factors in their simplest, strongest form as love and hate. And now let it be said at once, and again in the simplest possible terms, that *when the infant encounters love he encounters God*.

The day of his birth, then, is the day of his first, and in some respects his greatest religious crisis. For on that day, and following it according as the lot befalls him, he encounters as much of love, or such kind of love, as his parents are adequate to give. To keep the religious terms, let us return to expressions in the Epistle to the Hebrews, as discussed in Chapter I. Love is what was called there an archetype. Elsewhere in the New Testament the same view is expressed by simply saying, "God *is* love." Perfect love, then, is of the cosmic or eternal order. That external love can be known in the earthly or natural order in many ways, running from the most perfect living of it to a badly distorted likeness to it.

Now much the same thing is true of parental love. We may admit with gladness that God is in that parental love. Yet we must also admit with honest realism that *man* is in it too; and so in consequence, the God to whom an infant is first responding, though unconscious and unaware of it, is distorted by the human prism as he reaches the infant. Thus the infant, it may be, is coming to know love, but love which is only a copy, or "shadow," or perhaps only a remote likeness, to eternal, perfect love.

Or the distance between perfect love and "love" as the child actually receives it may be greater still. He may be then given what is offered as love and received as love, but in reality is a substitute; not outgoing, self-giving love, but selfish love which holds the infant, dominates him, smothers him with spurious affection, and will not release him for growth. Or again he may encounter any of the other kinds of parental inadequacy already mentioned —rivalry between parents, partiality as between their children, poverty of emotion, rejection, hostility, or open hate.

By some of these, according to his lot, an infant is confronted, and out of these his own self creates the pattern and direction of its own dynamics. And *this dynamic self is the ground into which his next confrontation comes.*

As infancy passes into childhood and as the child begins to talk, he is confronted by what we may call the parental view of life. In families where husband and wife are virtually at one in their conscious view of life, the child encounters, as it were, a unified philosophy in the family from his earliest years. Where he encounters rival views of life, he will probably be influenced by the degree of closeness to the mother or father, as the case may be, but he is still left in tension by the necessity of siding with one parent's views and disvaluing those of the other.

In considering the endless number of views of life which exist, let us return to the terms used at the beginning of this book—life as treadmill, as saga, and as pilgrimage.

When life is felt by parents as treadmill, we must expect that the parental view of religion will be deeply colored by that fact. If religion is *valued*, it need cause no surprise if religion is sought as a means of escape from intolerable conditions, or as holding out the promise of compensation in a future life, or as furnishing tremendous emotional orgies, or as a means of assailing in the name of God the status of the privileged rich. But we must be prepared to recognize also that many to whom life is treadmill with all exits blocked, regard religion as "opiate," consider the church as enemy; and hold these views like a leaden screen between the child and God or between the child and the church.

Where life is felt by the parents as saga, religion again will be deeply colored, but probably with a different dye. For these are the folk to whom life is good, optimism is easy, and the world, if not the best possible world, is at least making rapid progress and will continue to do so if malcontents and agitators can only be kept in their proper place. It is quite possible, and very often true, that no need for religion is felt at all. Man is good, the prospect pleases, there is enough to eat and money is in the bank, Reason is God, power is the chief end of man, and expediency is the law of life. As long as business is good and health is fair, religion can wait.

If religion is valued by those to whom life is saga, it is not to be wondered at if religion is understood as a means of supporting and bolstering the kind of life in which such good privileges can be enjoyed. Religion which will play that role in society can be supported financially and morally, with confidence. Religion which demands more than that of man or society is intuitively felt as a threat.

And here, quite as truly as when life is treadmill, the parental view may intervene like a leaden screen between the child and God, or between the child and the church.

When life is felt by the parents as pilgrimage we are likely to find several characteristics, that is, marks of parental character. For one thing life is felt as existing both in time and in eternity. The result is a sense of proportion and of perspective which is difficult if not wholly impossible in a secular view of life. If the sense of time outweighs the sense of eternity, we bog down in mopping up after yesterday and getting ready for tomorrow. If the sense of eternity outweighs the sense of time the goal is set so far ahead that we become indifferent to the journey itself. In either case we forfeit *today*, the present. But when the senses of time and eternity are balanced we capture today. And in so doing we can then be given the saving grace of true humor. We can laugh, not with derision or cynicism, but with the kind of laughter which God is said to give,[4] the laughter that arises when we are able to see a distorted detail in its true proportion but under the divine perspective.

In this sense true humor nourishes the roots of true joy, as may be seen in the great poem, *The Magnificat,* where the pompous mighty have suddenly collapsed, the truly humble have been exalted, God's will is done, and the human instrument of that will can sing for sheer joy though knowing that pain lies ahead. This, it will be remembered, is given us as a mother's song,[5] and it is the absolute opposite of despair.

Again, when life is felt as pilgrimage, parents are found trying to do away with all sorts of barriers that shield man from knowing and receiving God, that they may the better commune face to face. This is more than what we commonly call prayer, although that is included. It is the desire that *God* may confront *us* as He truly is, with distorting filters and leaden screens done away.

And when life is felt as pilgrimage parents seek to place personal values above material values; and this is reflected in endless ways in their reaction to each other, to their children, to church, to work, business, government, and so on.

Thus in the degree to which life is felt as pilgrimage, the children are left open to religious confrontation with a minimum of distortion of that perfect love which reaches out, in these confrontations, toward man.

Now the dynamic self, being born *within* the actual relationships of a family group is also being born *into* the parental view of life. These two, the actual dynamic relationships with the parents and the parental view of life constitute, as it were, two filters, or even two leaden plates, through which eternal, liberating love must pass before it can penetrate to the core of the child's dynamic self. This is part of the reason for proposing the principle that the emotional life of the individual as infant and as child determines the kind of religion he *can* respond to and make his own. And this is one, though of course not the only, way of describing the human situation of the child when he begins to be confronted by the facts and the teachings of Christianity as they come to him in verbal form.

A child's next specifically religious confrontation, if indeed he encounters it, is formal religious teaching, and the church. These two have been well discussed in reference to children, in many books, so much so that we need not pause to consider them here except to state a few points for the sake of clarity. Through formal religious teaching at home and in church, the child is consciously confronted by God, by Jesus Christ as the living, personal Word of God, and by the Bible as the written word of God.

Through the church he is confronted by a society of persons who in principle are a larger family and who constitute the visible Body of Christ now living on earth. As with the child's parents, so, too, with the church which confronts him: it embodies the eternal love within the form of a human society, a love sometimes brilliant in its near approach to purity, but often a love which can be seen only in a dim glass, darkly.

And here, if we are to be as honest in regard to the church as we seek to be in reference to the parents, we must reckon with the sore temptation of any church to believe that it is perfect and infallible in its present form. The degree in which a church yields to that temptation may well be taken as a measure, not of its divinity, but of its humanity.

For the more stridently a church asserts its claims to be the only true church, the nearer it approaches to the role of the possessive human parent who professes to know all, can admit no error, knows what is best for a child, decrees what is right and wrong, pours out love on the child who conforms and opens the vials of its wrath upon one who dares to rebel.

For what the church may mean to a child is profoundly influenced by the view of itself which a particular society of Christians holds. It is readily seen that the church may be a mother to a child for a time, and supply deep needs which neither mother nor father can meet. But it is significant that in the Biblical view this is not conceived to be the role of the church. There the church is spoken of in many ways: it is a family, a household, a brotherhood, a body with its parts; and so on; but never in those writings is the church our mother, or our father.[6] After the earthly parents the role of parenthood in the eternal order is reserved to God and God alone. The extent to which this is recognized in a church and translated into the practices used in dealing with children will largely determine the degree to which the church either usurps parenthood and prolongs spiritual infancy, or begins to liberate a child into the spiritual freedom of the Christian society whose only spiritual head is Jesus Christ; and whose only spiritual Father is God.

These then, we may regard as being among the deeper spiritual crises of childhood: the kind of parental love, the nature of the parental view of life, the kind of formal religious teaching, and the kind of church which he encounters.

FAITH

And the nature of the dynamic self which he is becoming determines, we have already said, the kind of religion to which he can respond and make his own. His response is his faith, or his shrinking back, as his case may be.

What theology refers to as "saving faith" may begin at so early an age that no one dares to place its lowest limits in terms of age. If a child encounters warm and genuine parental love; if the parental view of life does not seriously distort the claims of God on human life; if the religious teaching presents Jesus Christ so as to awaken the response of love and trust; then who is to say how early a child may be of the Kingdom of God?

Yet it is easy to see, on the other hand, that in many cases the dynamic self, being what it is, may hold a child back from an outgoing response to religious teachings or to the church unless and until some fresh confrontation in later years disturbs or even shatters the existing self and sends it groping in hunger for what it has hitherto denied or rejected.

But in any case where faith can be said to exist we must reckon with all the possible discolorations which the dynamic self is capable of giving, for example to God, Jesus Christ, the Bible, the church, the church's teaching, and so on, as one encounters them.

This capacity of the dynamic self to select and distort the materials which one encounters in the religious confrontation seems to be rooted in childhood. Often we can see it beginning to operate in the early years in ways such as have been mentioned previously in this chapter. Thus, as already seen, a child who is emotionally deprived may, when he enters the church school, have difficulty in relating to other children, and may withdraw, or present behavior problems, or show affect hunger by seeking extraordinary attention, etc. That is, he is handicapped at the outset in entering into and participating in *Christian fellowship*, which is one of the distinctive characteristics of the Christian church. In theological terms this distinctive fellowship is thought of as indwelt by the Holy Spirit, and is of the eternal order. Yet here is a child, perhaps scarcely more than an infant, who, it may be, resists it, or disturbs it, or misunderstands it, because of the nature of his own dynamic self at the time.

In a similar way we might discover that if a child's relation with his parents is deeply disturbed the development of a wholesome conscience is prevented, and a lack of conscience, or an oversensitive conscience, or a rigid conscience may begin to be the result. In any such event any Christian teaching regarding conduct, sin, and forgiveness seems to be especially liable to distortion, or misunderstanding, or superficiality, from childhood on.

Here in childhood, then, when a child encounters the religious confrontation and responds to it, it is as if one of two kinds of faith begins to form: a faith which permits growth because it opens the self to God; and a faith which hinders growth because it functions in such a way as to seal off those very areas of the self which most sorely need God.

The former kind of faith, in turn, may, in mature life, constitute the basis for a spiritual growth which can move on toward its rich culmination and fulfilment; while the latter kind of faith may provide the basis for a distorted philosophy of Christianity and a disturbing kind of Christian experience which yields neither growth nor joy. To this we are to return in Chapter V. But next we turn to consider some of the crises of adolescence.

CHAPTER THREE

My Father's Business

THE DRAMA OF CHILDHOOD has its sequel in the drama of adolescence. In the former, the central problem was individuation. In adolescence the central problem is that of becoming psychologically weaned from the parents. The nature and degree of the weaning which is achieved during adolescence have much to do with the kind of growth which can take place within the adolescent years and with the later adequacy of the individual for the more mature responsibilities of adulthood.

ADOLESCENCE

It will be recalled that we spoke of the child as encountering the world of persons, of things, of gender, and of persons of the same sex. The child enters adolescence with whatever solutions and whatever blocking he may have already achieved, such as in his relation to persons, especially his own mother and father; in his relation to things; in his relation to himself as an "I" who knows himself, has a gender, and begins to pass moral judgment on himself through his conscience; in his relation to others of the same sex, and in his relation to authority.

He takes with him, too, whatever of faith or of shrinking back there may be in his response to love, to the parental view of life, to formal religious teaching and to the church. In short, the dynamic self which he has become by the time of adolescence moves on to a still broader stage. Whatever has been well achieved in his character is now his ally. What has been poorly achieved or blocked in character is his handicap until he can secure release.

It appears further, as we saw, that the most basic element in this dynamic self emerging from childhood is the relation with his own mother and father. And now the quality of that relation to the parents is to be still further tested by the manner and the degree in which he can wean himself from them. The test itself is presented to him in nature by two great confrontations during adolescence. Both of these are still essentially in the world of persons. The first is the world of persons of the opposite sex. The second is the world of history in the broadest sense, the present in its relation to the past and to the future. We may consider these in that order.

THE OPPOSITE SEX

Long before adolescence, of course, a child is conscious both of gender and of sex. During later childhood, however, it is common for boys to be indifferent or even hostile to girls, and vice versa. But with the onset of puberty the physical changes taking place in the body begin to be profoundly felt in the psyche. The new element that is arising *within* the dynamic self causes one to become intensely aware of the new element that is arising also *outside* of him in persons of the opposite sex.

Thus, and now in a new sense, deep begins to call to deep. The wonder and the beauty of this call which resounds through so much of animate nature touches one of the profoundest chords in man. In adolescence, youth begins intuitively to understand that in due time he must answer that call. Is his answer eventually to be a yes, or a no? And what manner of yes, or of no, is it to be?

As with gender, so with sex: it is from nature, but it is more. In its deepest aspects it is a religious confrontation. For as the question of marriage begins to become personal it is seen to involve two crucial demands upon love: a union, and a separation. Both these demands upon life are rooted in the religious conception of marriage: "Therefore shall a man *leave* his father and his mother, and shall *cleave* unto his wife: and the two shall be one flesh." [1] But it cannot escape notice that the demand to "leave" is prior to the demand to "cleave."

Now there is a sense in which the whole drama of adolescence, as far as one's relation to persons of the opposite sex is concerned, represents the anticipatory working out of an individual's struggle between two competing claims upon love, namely, the demand to continue to cleave to the parents, and the demand to be able to cleave eventually to the mate. So the adolescent crisis in the emotional life is a crisis, not merely of a particular episode, but rather it is a crisis extending over several years during which he becomes prepared to solve in some fashion the rival claims of the parents and of the mate, for the deepest love which he is capable of giving.

We may think of the drama of adolescence as having three acts embracing the periods of early, middle, and late adolescence respectively. As far as ages are concerned, the first act corresponds roughly to Junior High School, say about twelve to fourteen; and the second to Senior High School, say fifteen to seventeen. But, as we shall see, the third act is often greatly prolonged.

In typical American families a youth is living with his parents during the first and second acts, and perhaps during the third. Commonly he is more or less dependent on them economically. His capacity to release himself psychologically *from* the parents and *toward* persons of the opposite sex cannot be known until the third act or even later. But during youth one may discern certain general types of response which suggest how the struggle is going at a given time during the second or the third act. Four such types will illustrate the point. First, there is the youth who is able to relate easily to many persons of the opposite sex. Basically secure in his own emotional life, he does not have to bid for warmth of feeling by offering either things or sex in return for friendship.

Young people are intensely aware of the value of such a personality. They often express it by saying such things as, "He, or she, can make friends because he can be a friend." Having many friends, he is the more prized as a friend. If he is capable of relating deeply as well as easily, falling in love can be more than a matter of accidental nearness; it can also truly involve the element of choice.

2   Then there is the affect-hungry boy or girl. Not having experienced deep and sufficient love in the earlier years, in adolescence it is easier to confuse the desire for physical expression with love, of which it may become the deepest symbol. Not being basically secure in one's own emotional relations it is easy to bid for love with the symbol of love. Lonely, and inexperienced in deep, healthy human relations one may easily mistake passion in the partner for love, and regard a promise as evidence of sincerity.

Some so situated snatch very young at marriage as an escape from intolerable home relationships. Others may be drawn irresistibly into sexual relations before marriage. Some are left as stranded victims of pregnancy or disease. Still others, insatiable, run the gamut of every conceivable physical expression, burning with lust but never knowing love. If one is to place any confidence in such widely publicized statistical studies as those of Kinsey and others, he is fairly entitled to read the results as being partly a symptom of emotional starvation in the earlier life of American youth.

3   Again, as a third type, there are the youths who continue to keep their friendships largely or wholly within the limits of their own sex, boy with boys and girl with girls, during the second or even the third acts of the drama of adolescence. And as a fourth 4 type there are the youths who have few, if any, friends either among their own or the opposite sex.

In any case where youth holds back from warm and natural friendships among the opposite sex the reasons may be obvious or they may be obscure. The most obvious reason in many instances is lack of opportunity for knowing many persons of the opposite sex. This condition often exists in the country, in sparsely settled areas, in small towns, and is deliberately fostered in those high schools and colleges which are based on the segregation of the sexes. The more obscure reasons are often of an intensely painful nature, such as anxiety over one's physique, his clothes, his family standing, attitudes, or traditions, his own occupation, and so on. But whatever the reasons, our chief point just now is that in these cases the youth is held *toward* his parents and *away from* persons of the opposite sex, at least for a time.

THE WORLD OF HISTORY

The second great confrontation of the adolescent to which we referred, is the world of history. By "history" we do not mean simply the subject which is given that title in the school curriculum. We mean, rather, the total stream of man's experience and achievement as it surrounds us in the present; as it comes to us out of the past; and as it bears us onward into the future. "History" in this broad sense includes, for example, the culture we live in; the visible evidences of our strivings as seen in homes, cities, industries, and government; our sciences and our practical technics for getting things done; the literature and the philosophies which we keep alive; interpretations of the past which we commonly call history; the traditions which we cherish; our interpretation of the present world scene; the dangers we regard as most threatening; the attempts we make to foretell the future; the measures we count on to protect us in the future; our religions with their past, their present, and the goals they seek in the future; and so on.

Obviously history does not wait until adolescence to confront the individual. But the adolescent is confronted by history in two forms which are especially significant to him at that time in his life. The first of these is family history which confronts him in the form of the traditions, the values, and the pressures of a particular family. The second is the broader world of history, or as much of it as youth encounters in Junior High School, Senior High School, and college. These two forms in which the world of history confronts youth should be separately considered.

FAMILY TRADITIONS

In the preceding chapter we observed that an individual encounters the parental view of life while he is still a child. The parents, for their part, may feel themselves to be within a longer family line, reaching back generation after generation with the accumulating traditions and the cherished values which happen to belong to a particular family line.

Family traditions vary greatly, of course, and individual parents vary just as greatly in the value or the lack of it which they attribute to a family line. But in many cases as a child enters adolescence it is as if the parental view of life with its pressures upon the young now begins to be reinforced by the longer family view of life with still greater pressures— "You don't dare do that, James, because, remember, you are a Purvis"; or, "Son, I must say I am shocked at the interest you are showing in that Weisser girl. Remember, you are an Andrews"; or, "I am pleased with your record this term, but I am sure you can do better. Remember—"; or, "I can't imagine what's getting into you, son. Whoever heard of a Cosman holding views like that. It sounds to me perfectly scandalous to hear any member of *our* family talk like that!"

The strength and the persistence of family tradition can be well seen in concrete instances. This may be done by examining actual transmitted patterns of family life. By "transmitted patterns of family life" we mean some observable, definable way of meeting life which appears, more or less unchanged, generation after generation within a family line. When we seek our illustrations we shall begin with such patterns as may be discerned in two generations, then in three generations, and so forth. Obviously it is easiest to find material where only two generations are concerned, since parents and children living together in one household are so common a feature in our ordinary life. It will be increasingly difficult to find our material as the number of generations increases, for the reason that intimate and detailed knowledge of any one family line becomes more difficult to obtain in proportion as the number of generations increases.

The case of patterns transmitted through two generations could be illustrated in an almost endless variety of ways. As one example we may take a case which recently attracted wide attention. The newspapers carried headlines to the effect "Hungry Babies' Mother Gives Two Away on Street." One is first disposed to exclaim, "An unbelievably inhuman act!" But suppose we look behind the scenes. Linda Jones, the young mother in question, had been in love with Ernest, but Ernest went to sea and Linda married Edward. Babies came rapidly and, unable to assimilate the new responsibilities, Linda left her husband and turned the babies over to someone else to care for. Then Ernest returned, sought out Linda, and persuaded her to marry him. We cannot here go into the details of her somewhat frantic search for a way by which she might be free of the responsibility for her own children. The description of the mother as seeking to give away the children is only a newspaper man's way of describing an end result which had been reached at a given moment.

But why was Linda this kind of person? We cannot answer that inquiry fully but it must serve our purpose at this moment to say that her family was that kind of family. They had met life partly by running away from it and placing the responsibility on other shoulders than their own. The records of the relief agencies of that community could give the details abundantly, for there were fourteen agencies which had known and helped the family for fifteen years and, in six of these years alone, one county had given this family $2,500 to say nothing of what had been done by other agencies. This, then, looks like a pattern of evading life which appeared in two generations.

A pattern of a very different kind transmitted from one generation to another has been called to our attention recently by the work of Terman and by that of Burgess and Cottrell.[2] The former attempted to study psychological factors in marital happiness by statistical methods, and the latter attempted to use Terman's results, and those of other students of the subject, as a means for predicting marital happiness. These men have given us the fascinating generalization that "happiness runs in families." By that they mean to say that if a given couple are happy in their marriage, the child of that marriage stands a much better chance of making a happy marriage than is the case with a child of parents whose marriage was unhappy. It hardly need be said that this is no iron-clad rule, for of course there are exceptions; nevertheless these students of the family are convinced that the child of a happy marriage is likely to make a happy marriage for himself.

Then we have the case of patterns of family life which are transmitted through three generations. Illustrative material is very abundant in the records of clinics and in the records of social agencies. Nothing is more apparent in records of this kind than the depressing uniformity with which they make it clear, again and again, that a family has been ailing in some fashion, in the person of one or more of its members, for at least three generations. The records might show transmission for a much longer stretch of time than three generations, if the pertinent material could be gathered; but commonly the investigators limit themselves, for practical reasons, to three generations.

A case which exemplifies transmission through three generations with the possibility that it may involve four generations, is to be seen in a family whom we may call the Jacksons. Oliver Jackson, a boy of about fourteen years of age, is said by his mother to be on the point of making his profession of faith and coming into full membership in the church. On the day appointed for this profession, the Jackson family do not show up. No word of explanation is sent to the minister, but a few days later he hears to his great surprise that Oliver has run away from home, and has attempted to reach a state which is about 1,200 miles distant from the city in which the Jacksons now live. The minister visits the family, hearing a tale of woe poured out by Mr. and Mrs. Jackson, during which Oliver is described as a rebellious boy, difficult to manage, and frequently in trouble. The limits of the minister's ability to aid this family in its internal problem are soon reached and the family wisely turns to a mental hygiene clinic for further help.

In the interviews at the clinic it becomes apparent that a deep hostility exists between the mother and the son, and that Mr. and Mrs. Jackson themselves are in difficulties in their relationship with each other. Mrs. Jackson has not been able to accept her own son with simple, warm, genuine, and deep affection. As the interviews progress it becomes evident that Mrs. Jackson stood in a similar relation to her own mother, to whom she still feels a hostility so great as to frighten her.

During the interviews with Mrs. Jackson the fact is brought out that she, as a girl, turned to her grandmother instead of her mother for the emotional support and counsel which under favorable circumstances she would have received from her own mother. We are left to guess whether Mrs. Jackson's mother had emotionally rejected *her* child, the present Mrs. Jackson; and we are left also to guess whether Mrs. Jackson's mother may, in her turn, have been emotionally rejected by *her* mother, the grandmother of Mrs. Jackson. Some of the evidence supports the conjecture that this was the case.

Whether the conjecture is correct in this instance or not, it is true that in comparable cases a pattern of maternal rejection may be traced as it does its devastating work in three or even four generations, sometimes leaving in its wake as many generations of damaged human lives. And it is important for our purposes to remember that in many instances the persons thus damaged in their living, may turn to the outward forms of religion as a way of supporting themselves in an intolerable situation.

A heavy reliance upon the outward forms of Christianity is evident in the Jackson family. Mrs. Jackson is intensely religious, with the kind of religion which is rigid in its insistence upon correct beliefs. We have some traces to indicate that a similar kind of religion was practiced in the family from which she sprang, for the grandmother's religion is described as being of the same kind.

Again there are records to indicate the transmission of family patterns through a still greater number of generations. For example, *The Adams Family* by James Truslow Adams traces the history of that eminent family through at least four generations. At an opposite pole, Harlan W. Gilmore has studied the Jed family which produced a series of beggars through at least five generations.[3]

But records of the type we have just been citing still fail to bring out the nature of the inner struggle as the adolescent tries to work out a solution between the various competing demands of the family tradition, on the one hand, and his own developing individuality, on the other. For the purpose of understanding the inner struggle our best resource is great or near-great literary fiction. Fortunately this problem of transmitted family patterns and the resulting struggle has occupied the attention of many modern writers whose work has much psychological value.

Among works of this kind we may mention Thomas Mann's *Buddenbrooks;* "The Forsyte Saga" by John Galsworthy in four novels entitled, respectively, *Man of Property, Indian Summer of a Forsyte, In Chancery,* and *Awakening;* Sigrid Undset's "Kristin Lavransdatter" in three novels, *The Bridal Wreath, The Mistress of Husaby,* and *The Cross;* Daphne du Maurier's *Hungry Hill;* John P. Marquand's *The Late George Apley;* and Gerald W. Brace's *The Garretson Chronicle.*

The life stories so discerningly unfolded in these books go far beyond adolescence, happily. But in reading them one cannot miss seeing how painfully the adolescent struggles in working out a relation toward the sex code, toward property, and toward career; with family tradition pressing in one direction and personal inclination pressing in another.

THE SAGA OF MAN

And youth encounters the broader world of history, in the sense to which we have already alluded. He is being introduced to the Great Society of Man, with its present, and with its relation to the past and the future. The channels through which the great society makes its impact upon youth vary with the individual, of course. But one thinks especially of such common examples as the community, the school and the college or university, radio and television, movies, sports, newspapers, reading which one chooses for himself, travel, economic cycles, the clash of ideologies, strikes, laws, agents and agencies of government, and organized religion in its Jewish, Protestant, Roman Catholic and numerous other forms.

Running through it all is social stratification into caste and class.[4] And lowering over it all is war; war as a factor in the past, or war as present threat, or war as present experience, or war in its aftermath. Through these and scores of other channels the great society thrusts itself in upon a youth, requiring that he come to terms with this or that aspect of the total world of actual history.

In our opening chapter we called attention to the view of life as saga, that is to say, to a secular view of the world of history. And now we should also consider the pressure placed upon youth to orient himself by a secular view of life at the very period of his own existence when typically he is trying to wean himself from his parents and find a place for himself in the great society.

Secularism derives much of the weight of its pressure from its pervasiveness, for it invades every phase of life. Since it is so familiar, perhaps no one as yet is able to assess its true import in the actual world of history, or to say what is more and what is less significant among its influences. But out of all the pressures which secularism exerts upon youth, we may single out four that appear to have crucial significance in the development of the self at the time of psychological weaning. They are crucial in the sense that they present a crisis, or more correctly a series of crises, during the weaning period. For taken as a whole they press youth toward the goal of a self, a course of life, and a philosophy of the world of history, all conceived as moving strictly within the secular plane and limited to the order of nature.

One of these is the pressure of secular values. By its own nature secularism neglects or rejects the cosmic and eternal order as a frame of reference in arriving at a sense of values, and restricts itself to the order of nature, particularly to the here and now. But secularism itself is in conflict as to what the primary values are, within the order of nature. In its sharpest form the conflict is between humanism and materialism, human values and material values. In its confessions of faith, especially in the presence of the young, secularism often puts human values uppermost, for example in such terms as human freedom, human happiness, peace, welfare, health, and so on.

But in practice, and again in the presence of youth, secularism often reverses the order, putting material values first and subordinating human values to such considerations as power, prestige, size of income, purchasing power, productive capacity, markets, and the like. A common theme is, "Make money. Make it honestly if you can, but make money."

Thus as a youth seeks to wean himself and enter a little further into the great society he finds again, but now on a wider scale, the same kind of situation which he encountered as an infant, namely, the offer of *things* as a source of security and power when the capacity for love is running dry. This atmosphere surrounds him as he sees people carrying on their daily affairs, and as he seeks to choose his own vocation.

Another pressure is that of secularism in education. We are not referring now to the separation of church and state, nor to the consequent development of two systems of education, one called secular and the other called religious. Rather, the feature of the present situation which here claims attention is the pressure of secularism as felt in *all* education. For it would seem that secularism tends to invade *every* kind of education, whatever label the particular branch or level or type of education may happen to wear, and whether offered by the state, or the church, or private individuals, or chartered corporations.

In the extent to which this is so, the young are kept preoccupied with objects, facts, problems, processes, interpretations, advantages, and so on, which lie within the order of nature. To that extent it can be said that secular education is education in naturalism, whoever conducts it. And by the same token and to that same extent the young are screened off from awareness of the cosmic and eternal order with its claims upon human life.

A third pressure upon youth is that of secular authority. As a youth seeks to wean himself from his parents he finds himself confronted by numerous portions and representatives of the great society who claim authority over him and press their demands upon him. Here we limit our thought to the authority of the state. It is true we are now considering the case of youth who are not yet "of age." But modern history has shown how quickly the state, or even a mere handful of men, can sweep the youth of an entire nation into any frame of mind or any course of action.

The underpinning of the secular authority of the state lies in the sense of nationalism and patriotism. The nation, as one portion of the great society, is presented to youth as the *patria*, the personalized "Father" land or "Mother" land. Typically it takes on some of the characteristics of a father, writ very large. Youth is taught that it is the nation which has produced us and nourished us. The nation gave us our advantages, guarantees our liberties, and provides for us in our emergencies. It protects us from our enemies and we must protect it. The nation is all powerful, has a glorious tradition, and has never been seriously in the wrong.

And the young are taught that to the *patria* we owe *patriotism*, that is, love, loyalty, obedience, and conformity, not now such as a child owes to a father, but such as a citizen owes to a sovereign. For the national state confronts youth as his sovereign within the great society.

Four instruments of persuasion in support of secular authority are secular education, propaganda, law, and sanction (force, fine, imprisonment, or even death). These are by no means at the same level of approach to the human mind. But note especially how the role of secular education fluctuates. In time of peace secular education can employ a large degree of objectivity in interpreting the state to the young. But in times of great stress secular education, as far as it is under state control, lies in ready reach of those who make, interpret, or administer law, to be used in support of what is considered patriotic and to be purged of what is considered subversive. But whatever the instruments used, no one knows better than modern youth the agony of the conflict engendered as he senses that the sources of knowledge are drying up and that the state is beginning to move in to take over his mind. Nor does anyone know better than he the ecstasy of the final surrender of the self to the state as to a god.

The state, restricting itself to the secular plane, cannot use the eternal order as a frame of reference, but only the order of nature, in determining and judging its own authority. Thus secularism becomes a rounded-out system, complete within its own plane. Outwardly it is expressed through the values which determine decision, the education which interprets the world of history, and the authority which the state exercises over people. Its underlying philosophy draws heavily upon humanism, materialism, naturalism, nationalism, and patriotism. All, both expression and philosophy, lie within the order of nature.

The system is self-contained, and the authority is self-determined. Hence the way is left open within the secular plane for the national sovereign state to take on the role of God, determining the destiny of people. As long as things go well, the system is considered self-authenticating, and the future is bright. But if the system threatens to collapse, no further way to correct it from within has as yet been found.

Precisely at this point lies a major crisis for modern youth. For just as he is being introduced to the great society in order that he may take up a mature role in it, the system upon which that society has so painfully built up its gains in the secular plane threatens to go down around his head in chaos.

We who live in the western democracies and have passed the period of youth are caught in exactly the same dilemma, a fact which only makes it the more difficult for us to offer counsel, or for youth to find their way in the crisis. Take it, for example, from the point of view of American citizens of middle life or beyond. We have known a way of life in a political democracy, to which we are profoundly devoted. We love the land of our birth or of our adoption, love it so deeply that we are half afraid to voice that feeling, lest it be reckoned to us as cant. We abhor all totalitarianisms, whether Nazism, Communism, or what not. When organized forces of that stripe encroach upon us or threaten our freedom, every instinct of resistance and defense is aroused.

And yet that very devotion to our own way of life, and that very desire to preserve it, play relentlessly into the hands of nationalism, militarism, and jingoism. Our devotion to a way of life becomes devotion to the nation which feels itself threatened and determines to protect itself at any cost. We are committed to the nation, and the nation commits itself to a course of action in relation to other nations. Slowly, inexorably, we find ourselves being dragged to the edge of another abyss, a world conflict against which every fiber of our being protests but from which we can find no way to draw back without being traitors to the political values which we cherish.

In such a case how can we who are older be true to those who are younger? There are few in mature life who do not know the agony of that Gethsemane. But how, in point of fact, are we solving the dilemma? By making secularism into a religion to which we turn for deliverance from the very ills which secularism has bred.

For notwithstanding what is before our eyes in the modern world, the next pressure to which youth is subjected is the pressure to make secularism serve him as a religion. Secularism has many of the marks of a religion. It is the cult of the Kingdom of Man, propagated not by the church but by the state. It has its object of faith, which is Man. It has its theory of salvation, namely, redemption from our ills by means of progress,[5] intelligence, and the use of reason as best exemplified in scientific method. It lays upon youth the demand for supreme devotion to the state, especially in time of war. It has its orthodoxy expressed in political terms, with an elaborate machinery for running down heresy, and its system of discrediting and punishing the disloyal. It has its missionary enterprise; to democratize the world, if one is of the West; or to communize it, if he lives behind "the iron curtain." It holds out the promise of heaven when the world shall have been thoroughly democratized or communized, according as the state of blessedness is conceived. And it looks with shuddering gaze at the final conflict when the two rival heavens shall go down into Armageddon to do battle with the unleashed sword of the atom for the supremacy of the earth. For as if making an ultimate declaration of secular faith in the source of salvation and power, the awestruck mind now peers into the atom, rather than into the cosmos.

The plight of a youth consists partly in the fact that he knows, as if by intuition, that the demands laid upon him by this religion of secularism are shot through with evil; yet as long as he himself functions only within the secular plane he lacks a standard of reference by which to understand why they are evil. But if he tries to exercise his intuitive judgment, he is called a rebel. His plight consists partly also in the fact that the secular school and the secular state, by their own inner nature, serve as a screen to cut off from youth the view of life which would provide the point of reference for judging demonic elements which lurk in the secular view of life.

Now, it is the function of a spiritual religion to deliver man from precisely such predicaments as these. Let us turn then to consider some of the specifically religious confrontations which come to youth.

THE CHURCH

In the world of history the church exists, and there it confronts youth. While yet a child one may have known the church as an integral part of life, or as a casual part of it, or the church may have had no part at all in life as the youth has known it. But now as he enters adolescence the church takes on a potentially new and deeper significance, for reasons which lie very close to youth's own personal situation.

For note, in the first place, that youth is in danger of being caught in the grip of an iron-clad determinism and borne along by such forces as we have just been discussing. Many of the young feel this so keenly that they yield to a sense of a fate which they cannot alter and cannot avoid. For outwardly he is beset by heavy pressures to conform to the parental view of life, to the family traditions, to a secular view of life, and to the demands of the state.

Inwardly he is under pressure to wean himself, and assert his own individuality further than he was able to do as a child. But he is not certain what his own individuality is. And unless he can be helped toward a deeper self-discovery he is in danger of being swept along either toward a sterile conformity to the heaviest pressure, whatever that happens to be; or else toward a futile rebellion against all pressures from every source. In either case there is the possibility that a youth may become a sort of chronic adolescent, engaging hectically in living, yet stalemated by life; wanting more education, yet resisting it; resentful, yet still remaining dependent; growing older but not growing up.

But one is to be reminded, in the second place, that the grip of determinism is to be broken, not by exerting still heavier pressure from without, but by the formation of a new self within. Such a new self is not the result of a mere compromise between existing forces that play on one from without. It is a new force itself, which has come into being. In evolutionary terms it is a new emergent. In religious terms it is a new creation.

A new self is called into being by love. This ultimate fact in human experience was foreshadowed during childhood and youth, in one's relation with his parents, as far as may have been true in any given case. Later it may also be foreshadowed even more richly in one's own marriage. Yet at its best it is and must be love foreshadowed, not perfect love. Of this we spoke in the preceding chapter.

But now in youth love, not love foreshadowed but perfect love, confronts him from outside the secular plane, as God. But as with human love, so too with the love of God in yet another respect: it cannot attain its highest creativity until it is responded to. That is to say, the path to the deepest self-discovery and the utmost self-release lies within the two-fold experience of knowing oneself loved with infinite love, and of giving love in return "with all the heart, soul, mind, and strength."

Thus the deepest that is within the universe is calling to the deepest in youth. It is the role of the church to present this call to youth as fact, as promise, and as claim. And in responding, the way begins to open, out of natural determinisms, and into free citizenship in the eternal order.

The central facts of Jewish-Christian religious history illustrate this love of God, and this release of man. The principal symbols of thought in that same historic stream set forth the varied mean-

ings of human bondage, divine love, and divinely wrought redemption and release for man. For Protestant Christianity both
the redemptive act of God *for* man and the claims of God *upon*
man are expressed through Jesus Christ. As the living and personal
Word of God, he is set forth as coming out of the eternal order
into the order of nature and time. The Cross stands as the utmost
act of going down into the abyss of death with and for his beloved,
in an act done once in time and yet valid for all eternity. The
Resurrection stands both as example and as pledge of a spiritual
power able to shatter the determinisms of life and even the determinism of death itself.

The Gospel is proclaiming that these things are a fact, not a
theory. They do not confront us for discussion, but for response.
For the Gospel, further, is proclaiming that the Kingdom of God
is at hand, is here, to transcend the Kingdom of Man. It is a promise that these events of radical renewal and release, which happened
once for all, can happen again for any.

All these meanings are caught up in the great confrontation
which the church presents to youth in the Person, the message,
and the mission of Jesus Christ. And faith, put in the simplest terms,
is the outgoing of human love in response. Here, then, if the responding love is genuine, a new self is being born or is at least struggling to be born "of the Spirit."

The new self that is struggling to be born is struggling to enter
a new dimension. One is struggling to attain a standing point from
which to meet the conflicting claims which life has placed upon
him. Religious thinkers have long known the high significance of
this epoch in a human life when the soul is struggling to get free
of entanglements and contradictions and plot a new course of its
own choosing. In Christian thought this experience of shaking
off entangling hindrances and enlisting with the soul's own chosen
Sovereign is viewed as being a human terrain where it is one of
the special prerogatives of the Spirit of God to work for the
good of man. So the youth, struggling to free himself, struggling

to become a self, and seeking for an object worthy of utmost devotion, is seen as the object of divine compassion and divine assistance.

THE KINGDOM OF GOD

In religious terms the person who responds to the call of the Spirit enters the Kingdom of God. We should distinguish between the Kingdom of God and the church, for he will probably be a member of a church. The church is a society of persons, variously defined according to the polity of the particular communion. The Kingdom of God is here understood as a relationship between God and the individual in which the sovereignty of God over the whole of life is asserted from the one side, and either acknowledged or rejected on the other side.

The church involves the authority of man over man, an authority variously conceived in the different branches of Christianity, but an authority of man nonetheless, and very responsive to the patterns and pressures that happen to prevail in human society. But the Kingdom of God has to do with the authority of God, and of God only. If the two concepts, Kingdom of God and church, are allowed to become indistinguishable, the pretensions and tyranny of the church may become more intolerable than those of the state.

The Kingdom of God is claim, then, as well as promise; the claim of the sovereignty of God over the individual. The church presents this claim to youth. And see again where this finds youth. The claims of his parents and of his family traditions tend to hold him within the family pattern. Tending to wean him from the family dominance are the relationships with the opposite sex, the anticipatory claims of love between man and woman, and the claims of secularism heading up eventually in the demands of the national sovereign state.

Now where among all these claims upon him, is youth to reckon the position of the claims of the Kingdom of God? For this "Kingdom of God," let us be reminded, is the kingship of God, the sovereignty of God, and as such is a standing claim upon human love, loyalty, and obedience. But what then? Is this merely one more claim to be added to the many claims that already burden and distract the young? Or is it a claim which transcends all other claims of every sort, serving as a standard of reference by which all other claims of every kind may be tested?

In point of actual fact, for a given individual it may be either of these; one claim among many, or the supreme claim by which to orient oneself with regard to all other demands. Psychologically viewed, the problem is one of the individual's relation to authority. The individual's ability to solve the problem of authority at the religious level is affected by the nature of his relationship to human authority, especially the authority of parents and of church.

The principles that operate seem to be of this kind. In proportion as the individual is weaned from his parents he is psychologically free to admit the absolute sovereignty of God over the self. In proportion as he remains psychologically unweaned he tends unconsciously to identify *church* and *God* with *parents* or even with *one parent;* and then he tends to respond to the authority of the church or of God in a manner which befits his deepest feelings toward one or both parents. Thus the patterns that are possible in the response of youth to the claim of God upon human life are very numerous. We may take four, which are common, as illustrations.

The first may be called a change of sovereignty. The change is from an external to an internal authority, and from a human to a divine authority. This does not necessarily mean disavowing human authority, such as that of parents, state, or church. But it knows a hierarchy of authority, wherein the authority of God is supreme.

This is well and yet simply exemplified in the human development of Jesus. We are shown that at the age of twelve he could speak of "my Father's business," in a setting where the claims of "my Father" were already ranked by him as superior to those of Mary and Joseph; and yet this is no prig who evades plain responsibility under the guise of piosity, for we are also shown that he was "subject unto them." [6]

And the principle of the change of sovereignty is symbolically expressed in the act of publicly professing faith in Jesus Christ as Lord and Savior. Where the symbolic expression corresponds to the inward experience, the Christian goes literally and consciously under the sovereignty of God, seeking to govern all of life accordingly. Such a person, by acknowledging his supreme allegiance, has found a principle by which to judge between competing claims. This does not mean that the choice between competing claims is easily made; on the contrary, the suffering entailed by some of the choices may carry one out to the limits of endurance.

Nevertheless such a person has found a new dimension for the soul; and standing in that dimension, he is no longer at the mercy of the strongest pressures of the secular plane. These are the people whose final sovereign is in the eternal order, whose experience of that sovereign is an inward experience; and these are the persons, therefore, who are not long awed by human demands or tyrannies, whether emanating from parents, family, state, or church.

A second common pattern of response is that of external conformity. Here the motive is, "It is the thing to do." In this pattern youth may give assent to what is expected of him, as in making profession of faith or being confirmed, observing the accepted code of conduct, attending services of teaching and worship, and so on; while inwardly there may be indifference, or even active resentment, toward claims which one has not the heart to meet gladly, nor the courage to defy openly.

In many instances these are persons on whom the pressures of family and church, and perhaps of community as well, are very strong, and who respond to those pressures because to do so is the natural and easy course to take. But then this religion, adopted under pressure, is quite likely to be dropped as a burden. This dropping of the adopted religion may wait until the youth is away from home. But in other cases it may begin while he is still living at home, thus serving as a reprisal against a father or a mother who had, perhaps unconsciously, made religion serve the purposes of an emotional control over their children.

A third common pattern of response is that of rebellion. It can take the greatest variety of forms. It may, for example, be directed against the doctrines of the church, or some doctrine in particular may be taken up as a ground of offense. It may be rebellion against the church; the church as a whole, or some particular denomination, or some particular congregation; or the services of the church in general, or one service in particular, or some custom in the service. Or it may be rebellion against the Christian code of conduct in general; or some one item in the code of morals may become a symbol of revolt.

In all such rebellion we may not rule out the possibility that this is direct revolt against God and His claims on human life. But neither, on the other hand, may we lightly dismiss the possibility that rebellion in the area of religion is aimed at the parents more than at God. For rebellion against religion may in some instances be adopted unconsciously as a central measure in freeing oneself from parental domination, or perhaps as a means of making a parent suffer.

Suppose, for example, that a father is rigidly devoted to some particular article in a creed, an article which he regards as essential to salvation. Suppose further that this father is a powerful personality who seeks to dominate his son emotionally. In such a case the son may lack the courage to rebel directly against the father, but his attitude toward the crucial article of the father's creed needs perhaps to be seen as a symptom of feelings toward the father which can be best expressed indirectly. By rejecting or destroying what the father treasured, the son, it may be, is declaring a measure of independence, belittling an idol which the father had set up, and retaliating for suffering which a domineering father had caused. The variations on this theme which are possible, are almost limitless in number.

It should be clearly understood, however, that religious rebellion works in both directions; that is, there can be a rebellion of the young *toward* religion as well as against it. This appears to be happening to some extent at present in American life. For we find not at all infrequently that youth react away from a non-church family pattern, and seek in the church something which they have not found in their homes. And that, too, is seeking a new dimension in which to be about "my Father's business."

Then there is a fourth pattern, that of no response. This is the case for some because a religious interpretation of life and the religious claims upon life have never been encountered at all. For others, both interpretation and claim have left them non-committal. But in any event, these youth seek the fulfilment of life more or less completely within the secular plane, finding there, even in youth, a saga or a treadmill, as the case may be.

CHAPTER FOUR

He Was Tempted

YOUNG ADULTHOOD

As one leaves the period of youth he is confronted by the world of adult life, with its manifold responsibilities. He is placed under the demand to take up his own part as an adult in the emotional, economic, intellectual, social, and religious life of the world of his own day.

The personal situation of the young adult is shaped to a large degree by the nature and extent of the weaning which he was able to achieve during adolescence. In actual life there is every shade of variety in the weanings that take place. For the moment, however, we may think of those who are relatively well weaned psychologically by the time they have reached the early twenties, and of those who are not.

PROLONGED ADOLESCENCE

Those who have not achieved a relatively full weaning continue in a sort of prolonged adolescence. They may remain immature, for example, in regard to emotional responsibility, or economic responsibility, or intellectual or social or religious responsibility. There is a shrinking back from meeting and carrying some one or many of these responsibilities at an adult level, and a lingering on in some kind of dependency relationship. For one may continue to be a dependent in any or all of these areas for an indefinite period of time, perhaps for his entire life.

When the character development is arrested at the threshold of maturity there are two typical possibilities. One is that life's encounters will even yet take one irresistibly on toward maturity, leading him perhaps by the hard way into a ripeness of character not the less real because delayed beyond its appointed time. The other is that adolescence will become, as it were, a permanent state of mind beyond which no further advance will ever take place.

Many who study modern civilization are disposed to lay a large part of the ills of our time at the door of prolonged immaturity, and to regard the wider prevalence of maturity as a requisite for social salvation. When examined critically this turns out to be a secular thesis; for it finds both the ill and the remedy within the processes of nature. Maturity in and of itself is to be regarded as a healer. It is taken to be a necessary means of recovery from personal and social conditions which thwart and damage human life. That is to say, maturity, like reason and progress, comes to be regarded as means of salvation.

But when the inherent limitations of the thesis are understood, the fact that prolonged immaturity is so common still constitutes a serious indictment of our culture. It should be seen as a symptom of the sickness of a society if that society becomes so complex and so terrifying that the young lose heart for growing up and prefer instead to remain protected even at the cost of being dominated by parents or parental substitutes.

But let us now consider the case of those who have achieved enough of a weaning to permit them to begin passing beyond adolescence and toward maturity.

BASIC IDENTIFICATIONS

As one moves out of adolescence the central character problem is that of making the basic identifications around which his life as a mature adult can be developed.

It is well to be reminded why this is an essential stage in a developing life. As already observed, the central problem of childhood is individuation. That of adolescence is psychological weaning. Thus for some two decades the individual is forming. But in proportion as he is able to wean himself, a fresh crisis awaits him. That crisis turns upon the question: how shall the individuality and the freedom that have been achieved, be maintained? Will it be by *cutting* as many ties as possible? Or will it be by *forming* ties of one's own and maintaining them at a mature level?

ISOLATION

Many are greatly attracted by the first of these alternatives, that is, cutting as many ties as possible and forming as few as possible, in order to remain free. This has been a common response to life in modern times. For as the idea of individualism crept into common awareness it was widely recognized that the way to individuality was made vastly more difficult by old customs and conventions, especially in family life, political life, and religious life. Hence it came to be commonly believed that the way to become an individual lay along the negative road, that is, the road of *getting rid* of this or that encumbrance, whether in the person's immediate environment or in the total social situation. The solitary individual became something of a hero. Thoreau, living alone at Walden Pond, became a symbol of the self-sufficiency which many longed to have, the more so as civilization grew more complex, and as the leveling influences in democracy began to be more apparent.

So there began to be a cult of isolation. There was an isolation of the wilderness, such as that of Thoreau, and the Western settler who in folklore is said to live alone, talk little, and resent having a neighbor nearer than ten miles away. This escape to the wilderness was impossible for most, however, except in imagination, fiction, and the like. But an actual escape into solitude proved to be possible in the very place where the number of people was the greatest, that is, in the modern city. Here, if anywhere in the world, one could, if he wished, become anonymous, cut all ties, escape all responsibility, and "be himself" to his heart's content.

And then modern man was to discover that his isolation is more terrifying than the domination from which he sought to escape. This has come to be a common theme in recent times in literature of many kinds, but the intense feeling generated by isolation has nowhere been better expressed than by Dostoyevsky. Writing about 1880 in "The Brothers Karamazov," he saw even at that time the terrible isolation which results from an uncorrected individualism. One of the characters in this book is a man who has killed another many years ago but has gone undetected ever since. Now he is in a period of crisis as he seeks the solution for his own situation. Dostoyevsky puts the following words into his mouth:

Why, the isolation that prevails everywhere, above all in our age—it has not fully developed, it has not reached its limit yet. For every one strives to keep his individuality as apart as possible, wishes to secure the greatest possible fulness of life for himself; but meantime all his efforts result not in attaining fulness of life but self-destruction, for instead of self-realization he ends by arriving at complete solitude. All mankind in our age have split up into units, they all keep apart, each in his own groove; each one holds aloof, hides himself and hides what he has, from the rest, and he ends by being repelled by others and repelling them. He heaps up riches by himself and thinks, "how strong I am now and how secure," and in his madness he does not understand that the more he heaps up, the more he sinks into self-destructive impotence. For he is accustomed to rely upon himself alone and to cut himself off from the whole; he has trained himself not to believe in the help of others, in men and in humanity, and only trembles for fear he should lose his money and the privileges that he has won for himself.[1]

TEMPTATION

The alternative to cutting as many ties as possible is, as we have already observed, selecting, forming, and strengthening ties at the mature level. But while cutting ties may prove terrifying because of the isolation which results, the acceptance of ties may prove just as frightening because of the responsibilities which are involved.

By way of meeting such a dilemma the self may find some kind of compromise. A typical compromise for this purpose consists of striving to get that which we naturally and legitimately desire, but contriving to have someone else pay for it. The most serious temptations in young maturity, we may believe, have to do in some fashion sooner or later with this kind of compromise. For before the eyes of the young adult the shop window of modern life is filled with alluring goods; and over the window is spread the invitation, "Take what you want, and charge it to someone else's account."

This temptation is made the more plausible by the fact that other persons too have exactly the same natural and legitimate wishes as we. We can therefore identify with them, thus avoiding isolation; and at the same time we may lighten or even evade our own responsibility because someone else, or the group, or the leaders of the group, will see things through. *"They"* will pay. *They* will see that things do not go to pot.

All of this may be expressed by saying that the typical temptation of young maturity is the appeal to such identifications as promise to give what is legitimately wished, but to give it in such a way as to let the responsibility be shifted to other shoulders. And now in order to draw some of these threads together, let us consider certain major types of responsibility which confront the young man or woman. It will be observed that in each of these areas life presents an adult responsibility and offers a basic identification suited to that type of responsibility; and yet at the same time tempts one to shift the responsibility to other shoulders, thus leaving some aspect of character frozen at the level of childhood or youth.

EMOTIONAL RESPONSIBILITY

The deepest claim of life upon the individual is that he should give and receive mature love. Love at a mature level might exist between any two, but the love which especially concerns us here is the love of an adult for his parents, for his wife or husband should he marry, and for his child or children should he become a parent.

If one has been able to wean himself from his parents by the time he is an adult, his relation to his parents can be at a mature level. In that event the son or daughter can achieve many kinds of independence, and yet the relation with the parents can contain such qualities as affection, devotion, consideration, respect, emotional support, comfortable comradeship, and many more of the same kind. If necessary, economic assistance or even support can then be given in either direction, from parent to child or vice versa, without its being a threat to the relationship or a danger to self-respect.

If the weaning has not taken place in a wholesome manner, any of many possible results many follow. Two types are common. One is a severing of all relations, as far as that is ever possible. In that case the parent is felt as a threat even to the adult son or daughter, or vice versa, so that no warm and wholesome relationship is possible; and separating distance is desired by the son or daughter, or by the father or the mother, or perhaps by them all. Further growth of character is then impeded; and spiritual growth especially is rendered far more difficult.

The other familiar type of unweaned adult is the one who remains in too close a relationship to one or both the parents. This is the person who, though now "grown," continues to lean on the parents in some one or in many areas, such as the emotional, the economic, the intellectual, the social, or the religious. Very often hostility, more or less hidden, is a dynamic element in the relationships; and very frequently, too, these people are ailing in some sense, it may be physically, or emotionally, or morally or spiritually. All these unweaned adults, those who try to sever all connection with the parents and those who continue to cling too closely, may be said to have made a basic identification with their parents, which they cannot break.

The natural basic identification of maturity is in marriage to a husband or wife who also is mature enough to sustain the same role in return. In principle this is possible to those who are able wholesomely to break the basic identification with the parents and who have attained enough maturity to be able to assume the emotional responsibilities of a new basic identification. That is to say, we are dealing now with *the ability to enter marriage.* That ability, of course, exists in numerous forms and degrees, from which a few types may be taken as examples.

There is the individual who is emotionally adequate to enter marriage and to assume its responsibilities at a mature level. Given reasonably favorable opportunities for selecting a mate, such an individual is psychologically equipped to choose and to love a person who is mature enough to give mature love in return, and to accept the further emotional responsibilities of marriage as they arise.

Then there are those who are definitely inadequate to enter marriage. It may be that they have not solved the problem of gender sufficiently to make marriage a desired relationship. Or the reasons may lie elsewhere. But for the moment our chief point is that they are now predisposed to remain unmarried; and if pressed into marriage the result may be great unhappiness.

Again, there are those whose adequacy for marriage is not absent, but it has been seriously undermined. Numerous factors in modern life may damage one's adequacy for entering marriage without destroying it. Thus any forces which have the effect of prolonging adolescence may be counted on also to undermine adequacy for entering marriage. And here we should note also the effect of neurosis upon marriage. With the tendency of our culture to breed neuroses, the question of their effect upon marriage becomes a matter of great importance. Bergler, for example, in examining this question, has pointed out the tendency of the neurotic person to seek a neurotic mate, and thus to enter a marriage which, if it lasts, is held together not by mature love but by neurotic needs which are neurotically met.[2]

And there is the case of those who may be said to be inherently adequate to enter marriage and who have much to give, but whose marriage has been blocked by parental opposition. No one can ever know the stories with this motif which lie untold in the lives of many persons of middle age and beyond who have remained unmarried because they lacked the final act of courage needed to defy a loving tyrant. Henry James has treated this struggle of the domineering parent to prevent the marriage of a child, with great insight, in his *Washington Square*.

For those who marry, *the ability to sustain marriage* is a still more severe test of character than that which is involved in the ability to enter marriage. Here we touch two vast areas of human experience, namely, the growth of mature love within marriage, and the temptations to shirk the emotional responsibilities of marriage, leaving the partner to pay the emotional costs alone. Space will not permit considering these subjects separately, as they deserve; but they are deeply involved in the experience of parenthood, to which we turn.

The experience of parenthood is normally one of the major crises of life for both the mother and the father. It is a crisis in that it confronts them with a new life, new demands upon their love, new responsibilities, and thus with new tests of their spiritual adequacy for life's most basic physiological function, that of reproduction. For under the spell of desire a man and woman can physically procreate life in a matter of moments. But to give psychological birth to a new self and then to wean that new self into responsible maturity is a matter of years as far as time is concerned; and emotionally it is a vastly prolonged "labor," a labor of love and pain, of joy and of tears.

Knowing that this is so and sensing the cost without any unrealistic romanticism, there yet is the great company of those who accept parenthood as life's richest boon and through it enter ever more and more deeply into life. It is far below their due to say of them that these are the parents, but especially the mothers, whose sons and daughters hold the world together.

But, knowing the cost, there are those who shrink back from parenthood, deferring it year after year on this ground or that. And there are those who decide deliberately, not for reasons of health, that they will have no children. But in any case where the childless couple remain childless by deliberate choice it can often be seen that the passing years write their own slow judgment in the character structure of those whose long continued motive is to drink from the cup of life which they will not refill.

And there is the case of those who long for children, but know at last that they can never have them. The day when that fact is finally and irrevocably confirmed is a day of crisis too, for it is a day of the ultimate denial of an elemental desire. The impulses of motherhood and fatherhood need then to begin finding new channels, so that the springs of life may not start prematurely to dry up.

There are certain disruptions of family life, very common in modern times, which often disturb the growth of mature love between man and woman, and throw an unequal load of emotional responsibility on one of the married pair. Thus, for example, in war, to say nothing now of any other consequences, the separation of husband and wife puts both parties under a prolonged emotional strain which few can weather without scars. Where there are children, their care falls to one parent alone, distorting the psychic triangle. Marriages made during wartime commonly were followed shortly afterward by parting, subjecting both husband and wife to excessive strain without an accumulated fund of shared emotional experiences; and it was peculiarly difficult for the young wife, after a few weeks or perhaps only a few days of marriage to be left to carry, bear, and nurse a child in the husband's absence.

The family group may be disrupted by economic necessity, as when the father is away at his work for long periods, or when the mother must work away from home. Under these conditions one's emotional responsibilities can be carried only in a jerky manner. The pent-up feelings, both positive and negative, have to be discharged in too brief a time and in too intense a fashion, while long periods of emotional vacuum or even of resentment intervene between times.

Again, the family group may be disrupted by divorce. Here the growth of mature love as between man and woman is found to be impossible. If there are children, the parents find the growth of mature love toward the children made vastly more difficult in the divorce situation. In such circumstances the sense of emotional responsibility may, for example, be overdeveloped, or twisted, or atrophied.

All these types of family disruption, different as they are in other respects, have one feature in common and for the present this is the chief point. They make it the more plausible, and the more acceptable socially, for a young man or a young woman to enter into the emotional satisfactions of marriage without carrying to the full its emotional responsibilities.

ECONOMIC RESPONSIBILITY

In entering the world of adults one encounters the demand that he do his share of work, so as to support himself and contribute to the world's values.

An individual's sense of responsibility for work is one indication of the nature and degree of his maturity. For work is rooted in necessity. Thus, for example, work is an economic necessity; if the individual does not support himself or carry his fair share of work, someone else must do it for him. To the extent that he declines this responsibility, he is still at the nursing stage economically, living off someone else without contributing equally in return. Work is a psychological necessity, because it lies very close to the roots of self-respect; if one does not work he has in some manner to justify his idleness, to himself and to others. And work is a social necessity, because it requires work to enhance or even to maintain the world's stock of values, both material and non-material.

And because work *is* a necessity, the recognition of that necessity and the assumption of a responsibility are in themselves among the signs of maturity. For it is a recognition of reality, and it is a way of saying that one asks for no special favors.

But work is a problem as well as a necessity. It is so in many respects. Many cannot decide upon the kind of work for which they are fitted. Others know what they wish to do, but cannot find an opening in which to establish themselves in their chosen work. Then periodically there is no work of any sort to be found. Work is a problem again in that many kinds of work required in modern life are unrelieved drudgery, benumbing the mind and often impairing the body as well.

Work is a problem again in the sense that one of the deepest rifts in the modern world has to do, in part at least, with the nature of work and with the kinds of work which are to be counted as worthy of respect. Communism with its "labor theory of value" holds that the only true values are material values, and that the only labor worthy of respect is that which produces material values. With one breath it talks of a classless society, but with the next breath it sings a new aristocracy, that of the worker. On the other hand, democracy, without minimizing either labor or material values, knows a category of value which seems to be alien to communism. This is the category of non-material values, such as individuality, freedom of thought, freedom of speech, freedom of religion.

But work of many kinds has for centuries been identified with disadvantaged classes, while work of other kinds has been identified with privileged classes. And the tragedy of the case now is that the western democracies, although based to so large a degree on political and religious principles of the equality of persons, cannot even yet shake off the ancient distinctions between master and slave. So, in the democracies, one's work still tends to give him a basic identification with a class. The labels for the classes change from time to time, but at present are recognizable under such terms as workers, management, owners or capitalists.

In the area of economic responsibility the temptation is to avoid work for oneself and to live off the work of others in some form of dependency or exploitation. This temptation is the more subtle because there are ways of avoiding work which are respected and approved in one's own class, and this seems to be true no matter what the class to which one belongs.

Thus the "worker" can find the greatest variety of ways to squeeze his pay as high as possible, and squeeze his output as low as possible. The employer can be equally ingenious in finding ways to do exactly the opposite, that is, to squeeze the highest possible output for the lowest possible pay.

Or the temptation to avoid work may take still other forms. For instance, there is the temptation to avoid work altogether by living off society. Here the motto is, "Society owes me a living." And there is the temptation to live off the past, enjoying the returns from the accumulated labor and savings of other persons in other days.

Love and money are two of the mightiest forces known in man's life. The basic temptation is strikingly alike in both: Get as much as you can, and give as little in return as you can get away with.

SOCIAL RESPONSIBILITY

In speaking of social responsibility we have in mind the individual's responsibility as a member of a group. For the young adult is confronted by an almost interminable list of social groups within the great society. There are persons, of course, who seek to live wholly apart from any group identification. But if an individual is weaned from his parents his insufficiency emotionally and economically creates a powerful motive, perhaps an instinctive one, to identify with a group or groups. Let us here call identification with groups by the term "social identification."

Social identification becomes one of the major determinants in the development of character, partly for the reason that social responsibility can be developed and discharged in such a great variety of ways. A few typical patterns will illustrate the point, and will at the same time show a few of the temptations which lurk within social identification.

In one typical pattern of social identification the group serves as a haven. Here the individual seeks the group out of motives which contain a large element of fear in some form, such as fear of loneliness or distrust of one's ability to cope with the world. The group then may serve either or both of two purposes: it bolsters and supports the anxious self, and in it one can lose his identity in time of danger. The group then becomes a sort of Nirvana, or a social womb, into which the individual can retreat. "Belonging" in such cases means, to a greater or lesser extent, a surrender of will and conscience to the larger social self.

In another typical pattern of social identification the group attracts because it represents the self-interest of its members in a competitive society. Here the individual can take part in collective activity frankly designed to protect or advance the interests of one group within society, such as a particular class, or those following a particular trade or practicing a particular profession, or those engaged in a particular industry or line of business, and so forth. The motives of the individual often include a large element of aggression, retaliation, and the like which society would penalize if expressed individually, but accepts when expressed collectively.

In a third pattern of social identification the group serves as the vehicle for some particular type of social responsibility to the whole of society, or at least to some segment of it which is greater than the group itself. Here the motives are altruistic, that is, a disinterested seeking for the good of others through any appropriate channels. In this case the group represents the enlarged giving of the self.

Of course these are by no means all the functions of social identification. But these illustrations will at least suggest that the group meets many needs of the individuals comprising it, such as the need for withdrawal from life, or the need for aggression, or the need to express love on a widening scale. And broadly speaking any group may serve any of these three functions for a particular individual, although certain groups may by their own nature tend to serve one of these functions more than another.

But it is notable that the history of particular groups often reflects the same struggle which is so common in individual experience, namely, the impulse to express outgoing love for the sake of others, and at the same time the temptation to slip back to the level of self-interest. The first of these is illustrated, for example, in the case of many professional associations, such as societies of scientists and physicians, devoted to the discovery of truth and the promotion of human welfare. And in the political realm it has been strikingly illustrated by the emergence of two embryonic world groups, the League of Nations and the United Nations.

But the contrasted impulse to get everything possible for oneself is not only manifest in groups avowedly formed for purposes of self-interest; it is manifest also in groups professedly formed on an ethically higher level. Thus scientific and medical societies have discovered to their own dismay that their motives have to bear precisely the same scrutiny as do those of labor unions and associations of manufacturers. And as for the political world group, who needs to be told again of the surge of hope that greeted their birth, or of the grief that spread when nationalistic self-interest began to poison these children of the spirit?

And as for the young adult who enters any of the groups that surround him, his temptation is to let his groups serve the first or the second of the functions we have mentioned, rather than the third. That is, he is tempted to use his groups as a means of escape from individuality and retreat from responsibility, or as a channel for the pursuit of self-interest and the discharge of aggression. Now it is conceivable that all these are services needed by the individual under some circumstances. But if the group serves the individual in such a way as to help him hold back from the social expression of a mature, outgoing love, it has by that much helped him to remain immature and irresponsible.

INTELLECTUAL RESPONSIBILITY

In a democracy the individual encounters demands on his knowledge, opinion, and action in matters of general concern. If he is to be a responsible citizen it is incumbent on him that he bear an intellectual responsibility.

In the matter of knowledge concerning public affairs the ordinary adult is at a great disadvantage, for the issues are complex, and the information is abundant, but not readily secured; while much of the most vital information concerning matters of state, business, labor and religion are withheld from the public.

This being so, it is common for the individual to identify with some bloc in society. He tends to regard that bloc as a dependable purveyor of information, and is likely to shape his opinion by that which prevails in the bloc. It then approaches the impossible for facts or opinions of a different stripe to penetrate the minds of the adherents of a bloc. Partly for reasons of this kind we have the strange result that it is extremely difficult in a democracy, just as truly as in a totalitarian state, to know or to disseminate the truth regarding politics, economics, social conditions, or religious affairs.

The temptation for the individual is obvious: to surrender his mind and the directing of his action to his bloc. The principle is the same wherever the bloc exists. In politics, for example, one surrenders his mind and will, it may be, to one of the political parties, derives his political information from approved sources, then acts and votes along party lines. The same kind of surrender may take place to a bloc in economic affairs, or in social life, or in intellectual or religious life.

RELIGIOUS RESPONSIBILITY

As one enters the adult period of life he is confronted by the demand that he accept the responsibilities of religion and carry them at a mature level.

If his earlier life has anesthetized him against the claims of religion, it is to be expected that now he will continue to ignore its demands as an adult. It may be, however, that he will not ignore religion but will fight it. In that event it is always possible that the individual has not yet settled matters inwardly as concerns the claims of religion; his fight against it then means that he still is interested even though it is the interest of wishing to undermine or even to destroy religious tenets, a religious philosophy of life, religious institutions, or religious persons.

Or again, he may encounter some of the disturbing or shattering experiences of early adulthood which drive the self to seek for reorientation, or perhaps for rebirth and a wholly new beginning. Such a readiness for resurrection—that is, such a destroying of an old self with its complacencies—may come as a result of some overwhelming experience, as in times of personal tragedy, or family tragedy, or the social tragedies of war and revolution, and the like. In this event much of what was said in the preceding chapter is equally relevant here, for the individual of whom we are now thinking is seeking in adulthood rather than in adolescence for a way to break out of the determinisms which threaten to crush him, and is seeking to become a new self who can be free in spirit in any environment.

For the present we are thinking chiefly, however, of the person who has already made his initial personal commitment, as in a profession of faith or conformation, and who now faces the claims of religious responsibility as an adult. And we have to ask at once, what is the nature of religious responsibility? Here we have two great alternatives which, in oversimplified form, are these.

For one thing, religious responsibility may be understood as a responsibility which has to do with mature love and with the expression of that mature love in every area of life. That is to say, religious responsibility would then be conceived as reaching into the very realms which we have been discussing under such terms as emotional responsibility, economic responsibility, social responsibility, and intellectual responsibility. In that conception religious responsibility would have to do with every aspect of human life. Nothing in human existence, human relations, or human action would then be immune to the gospel of the resurrection of life.

In the second of the two great conceptions religious responsibility is coordinate with other types of responsibility and separate from them. It is one more responsibility added to other responsibilities. It is responsibility in a separate and peculiar category, not a responsibility which invades all other kinds of responsibility. Being a separate category added on to the rest of life it can be cultivated or not, as one may choose. But in either case religion, being separate from the rest of life, should stick to its corner of the arena and not get embroiled in the struggles which torment the rest of the arena. The upholders of this view may say to the minister, for example, "Your business is religion. Our business is business, law, agriculture, or what not. We want you to preach the Gospel to sinners for the salvation of souls. We will attend to business and politics."

It is of the greatest significance that Protestants once more are in the throes of deciding which of these two conceptions of religious responsibility shall prevail in the churches which in theory permit the greatest freedom of spirit. For many this turns out to be a painful decision, since the basic issues as to what the Gospel is and what salvation is are often clouded over by self-interest and uncriticized slogans, and not infrequently the young who are hungrily seeking a profounder faith are made to feel that they are placing their own souls in peril.

The basic identifications in religion we may take as being two: in relationship to God, and in relationship with the divine-human society, that is, the church. The first of these we have already considered in preceding chapters and we shall be returning to it in various connections later. Here we may think of the identifications with the church.

In identifying with the church and seeking to carry one's share of its responsibilities at a mature level, the individual is faced with a multitude of detailed questions and the necessity for practical decisions as to his share of work, his share in giving, his attendance upon services, his support of programs and policies, and the like. To brush aside such details as being of secondary importance is to reveal a rather impoverished conception of the nature of adult responsibility. One of the most obvious and frequent temptations of the young adult lies just here, namely, the temptation to accept passively the benefits and services of the church, but to let others carry the load and pay the price.

But there is another temptation of a profounder kind which one faces as he moves toward maturity, and that is the temptation to interpret religious responsibility in a way which will permit the individual to shield himself from the more searching demands of God upon human life. And it will be seen that the second conception of religious responsibility which we mentioned lends itself remarkably well to unconscious purposes of this kind. For if religion can be kept in a compartment to itself, separated off from our deeper feelings and emotions, from our political and economic affairs, from our social and intellectual life, then the demands of God upon the little cubicle that is left reposing under the suave label of "spiritual" will not be grievous. One can then occupy himself religiously with an abstraction which he fondly calls "the pure Gospel." By carefully controlling the terms used in defining "the Gospel" and "salvation" he can make sure that the religion which he approves will never lay upon him the demand of God that he change his human relations, nor his policies in business, learned profession, or labor union, nor his caste system, nor the way he uses his mind.

This, we believe, is the deeper temptation which faces those who arrive at the threshold of maturity in religion. It is the temptation to make religion his ally in shrinking back from the demands upon life which come to him out of the cosmic and eternal order and try to reach him through the Christian church.

Or to state the matter in a slightly different way: God seeks the individual through the church, but either the church or the individual may find ways to protect man against the demands of God. The church, using the simple process of defining itself and its mission, can shield man from the demands of God by means of verbal formulas. The individual, by seeking and supporting a theology which lends itself to his unconscious purposes, can interpose his theological formulas between himself and God so that the demands of God will not reach into his human relations, and the rest of his personal affairs. This is the man who then becomes very religious, it may be, but who in the hour of judgment cries out in consternation, "Lord, when saw we *Thee?*"

THE CONFRONTATION

Here, then, is the individual insufficient, with whatever pattern of dynamic self he brings with him into young maturity. He is confronted by the church with which he can make one of his basic identifications. The church, for its part, exists in a multitude of forms and varies greatly from one communion to another in the claims it makes for itself. But by and large we may say that in the church the insufficient individual is confronted by the moral demand of Christ: "Be ye perfect, even as your Father which is in heaven is perfect." This is the outward demand to fulfil one of man's profoundest inward desires, namely, the desire for moral perfection, that is, completeness or wholeness.

To some, this demand is as nothing. By the nature of the dynamic self in these cases, it may not even constitute a felt demand, because there is no awareness of a "Father in heaven"; that is, the orientation is wholly secular and there is no point of moral reference outside the self.

But for those who do hear it and for whom it *is* a felt demand, the demand itself is terrifying. Then, depending partly on the nature of the dynamic self which hears the moral demand and the nature of the church which presents it, the individual may find some manner of solution for his moral problem in the church.

The church may serve any of the functions described above; it may be a haven, or a channel for aggression, or a society where mature love can find expression. But there are two differences between the church and other groups which should be noted because they are especially significant in this connection.

The most important of these is the fact that it is the nature of the church to serve the third type of need, that is, to be a society in which mature love can be both received and expressed. This, of course, is exactly in keeping with the role of the church as a redemptive society.

And the second is that when a church slips below this level it carries within itself its own correction which is the demand for moral perfection, as expressed by and through Jesus Christ. Thus it has often been true that the church has been the scene of hostility and aggression which were expressed in the name of God. But any church which is not too greatly handicapped spiritually by dogmas concerning its own peculiar perfection in history and its infallibility in the present can recognize such episodes as being signs of spiritual degeneracy. A church which is thus spiritually free can confront its people who are seeking for moral growth, not with the myth of a historically perfect church but rather with the present fact of a morally perfect God.

The solution which the individual finds in response to the demand from within and without for moral wholeness may lie at any point on a long line of possibilities, ranging all the way from the vaguest compromise with God to the most radical remaking of the self. These varied solutions represent the equally varied *functional* meanings of salvation, that is, what salvation actually means to the individual in his present experience. In the attempt to sketch a few of these functional meanings of salvation, let us point to a few functions which the church serves, or may serve, in the lives of persons entering the adult years.

THE CHURCH AS HOME

The church may serve some of the most important functions of a home in the case of young men and women who are not married. Here one thinks of certain especially frequent personal situations.

There is the young unmarried adult whose life is crowded; whose human contacts are abundant, and who is enjoying the heady wine of physical maturity, good health, good status, and freedom to do as he likes. There is need for perspective in the midst of great activity, for help in keeping major and minor values distinguished, and for a sense of comradeship in the striving for a morally worthy life. These needs the church should be able to supply.

Then there are the young unmarried persons whose lives feel empty. In loneliness it is easy to give up the moral struggle and coast; for, "Who cares?" Here the simple yet profound need is for human comradeship and fellowship, not at the level of exploitation, but at that of genuine friendship. And this, too, it surely is part of the church's role in the world to supply.

In some cases, again, the need for human comradeship is even more urgent, for these people are not far from some form of inward disaster. In them the quest for salvation often is carried out in great agony of soul, for they frequently feel that they are doing battle against some terrifying threat, perhaps within themselves, or perhaps in the environing world, or in the church itself. Here the church often helps lives, that are seriously incomplete, to hold together.

In this service to these last two types of human need the church, if it fulfils its own inner nature, will differ greatly from many of the social groups which act as haven for the bewildered individual. In many groups of the latter sort individuality is lost. But in the church it should prove true that individuality is respected, honored, developed. And this is peculiarly important for the lonely person whose valuation of himself sinks lower and lower unless he feels himself genuinely valued by others.

To those in young maturity who find the church to be a home, the temptations are precisely those to which we have already alluded in speaking of religious responsibility. And the temptation of the church is of a similar kind—to let them remain immature, without responsibility, and without adequate stimulus to outgrow their spiritual adolescence or even childhood.

THE CHURCH AS ATTAINMENT

The ancient but ever-renewed predicament of man is reached again by any individual who feels the moral demand to be perfect, and who at the same time knows he is powerless to achieve that perfection. It is the function of Christianity to present to man a way by which he can surmount that otherwise overwhelming dilemma. In Pauline doctrine, and in those branches of Protestantism which understand and use the Pauline teaching, the solution is stated in terms of justification by faith.

According to that doctrine, by his faith the believer identifies with Jesus Christ, so that he is said to be "in Christ"; and he is accepted by God in all the warmth of a perfect Father-child relationship, not because he, the believer, is now a perfect person, but because of his identification with Jesus Christ. The doctrine of acceptance by God expresses in terms of theology precisely the same truth which we saw operating in a human family; namely, that the loving acceptance of a child by his parents is the only secure foundation for a healthy human self and for a wholesome conscience. But in theology the meaning of acceptance is put in a cosmic and eternal framework and deals with man's relation to God.

This Pauline doctrine of the divine acceptance on the ground of human faith in the divine Redeemer gives the profoundest possible solution for the problem of man's conscience under the divine demand; for it permits, or rather it invites, repose of spirit in utter confidence even while one is still embroiled in the moral struggle and while actual personal perfection of character is still far from being achieved. And the church, when acting within the great Pauline tradition, can offer what we may call spiritual attainment. It offers this spiritual attainment as the gift of God, and not as anything which is subject to human control.

But in the presence of this miracle of grace the church has shown a tendency to be as restless as the magicians of Pharaoh in the presence of Moses; she seems to feel that she, too, must present to man *her* miracle of healing the soul of man. That is to say, the church finds it surprisingly difficult to offer a Gospel whose power is all of God and is forever under the temptation to offer some kind of spiritual attainment or spiritual perfection which is subject to human control. Historically there are four types of perfectionism which have been common, reappearing again and again in various forms. Indeed, they have appeared so often that we may call each of them a tradition within the total Christian stream.

One of these is perfection of character. In this tradition, which began to form very early in Christian history, it is taught that per-

fect character can be attained during the earthly life. The terms
used vary, but it has been taught again and again in the name of
Christianity that the moral struggle can end by complete victory
over sin; while still in the human body one can be perfect, holy,
sanctified, sinless. Repose of spirit is offered then, in the present
life, as a blessing which awaits the successful outcome of the
moral struggle. In this tradition one is thought to be accepted by
God because he is a good man and deserves it.

A second persistent tradition is that of the perfect church. Here
a certain portion of the total company of Christian believers is
presented as the only true church. Man is then offered a peculiarly
favorable standing with God on condition that he enter the one
true church, or submit to it and entrust his eternal welfare to its
keeping. He is told, it may be, that salvation is not possible outside
this one true church, and that all others are heretics. In this tradition he is taught that he is acceptable to God because he is in the
only church that is acceptable to God.

A third persistent tradition is that of the perfect creed. Here one
is offered perfection of spiritual attainment in the realm of his
beliefs. One is a true Christian only if he subscribes to certain articles of belief. Faith then is not so much a matter of personal relation to God through Jesus Christ, as it is a relation to an objective
body of doctrine. In this tradition one is acceptable to God because
his faith is "sound," by which it is meant that he signifies his assent
to certain beliefs.

A fourth persistent tradition is that of the perfect Christian experience. In this instance the individual, at some crisis in his life,
has had an experience of divine grace which ever afterward seems
to him as his one glorious hour. It was so high an experience that
he feels he can never attain to it again, so perfect that he has no
hope of duplicating it, much less of ever transcending it.

He then begins to hark back to that hour as a kind of watershed;
he dates all events of the soul according as they fall Before Conversion or After Conversion, Before the Revival or After the Re-

vival; that is, before or after he experienced a profound sense of forgiveness, or an inrush of enabling power. But—and this is the spiritual tragedy of such a case as we have in view—he feeds upon his past, measures his present standing before God by his own "happy day," and basically lacks the faith to believe that a still greater measure of the same grace may yet be vouchsafed to him.

A friend who has called this tradition freshly to attention in the present connection, writes, "I once knew an old gentleman who gave a weekly testimony in a mid-week service. He told over and over of his conversion and how because of its new power he rushed out of the house and leaped over the fence. As I think back upon it, I think his leap was the last word in his experience. I used to wish he would tell us about getting on his feet and about further growth in experience."

Now each of these is in some manner a substitute for faith in Jesus Christ as the way of meeting the demand for moral perfection. They are a temptation to the church, because man can create and control them by the process of defining them. Then they become idols: the perfect character, the perfect church, the perfect creed, the perfect experience. In revering and protecting these idols of her own making, the church can then more easily put off facing the moral demands of a holy God.

And they are a temptation to the believer in that each of these idols is out beyond the self in the external world, where it can serve as a substitute for a relation with God in one's inner world. And so the Christian church, when its love of God runs low, repeats once more the old pattern which so many an infant first faced in his nursery: the offer of objective *things* as values, when the subjective reservoir of deep and simple love was empty. This, we may well believe, is one of the reasons why the younger churches, with nothing to offer but a transforming faith in Jesus Christ, spring up and sweep all before them.

THE CHURCH AS ENLARGEMENT

Again, the church serves a function which we may call that of enlargement. This, too, is brought about as a result of identification; for when the individual identifies with a group the self is in a better position to expand, both because of what the self does, and because of what is done to it, in the group. Thus we may speak not only of a dynamic self, but also of a dynamic group; and the dynamic group is capable, among other things, of strengthening and enlarging the otherwise insufficient selves who become part of it.

This function of the church as a group in the lives of persons coming into maturity is, or may be, of deep significance. It is especially so in two typical situations. One is the case of the young man or woman who senses an insufficiency in his personal life or in his marriage, but who is capable of rapid maturing of character even under great difficulties. In such a case the dynamics of group experience can often supply stimulations, support, and appreciations which would otherwise be lacking.

Another typical case is that of the young couple with their first child, or a family of young children. The experiences of parenthood are likely to stir up a sense of personal insufficiency in many areas of living, and the feelings of need aroused in early parenthood are among the most common influences leading young men and women to deepen or to renew their relationship with the church. To these young persons, then, the church may become an enlargement of their own personal selves, or of their family group.

The importance of this function of the church in the growth of the dynamic self can hardly be emphasized too greatly. It will be recalled that in Chapter III we spoke of transmitted patterns of family living. Had we carried the subject further we should have seen there is some reason to believe that families tend to run down morally and spiritually in successive generations unless replenished from sources outside the family itself. And it is the function of the church to be precisely that sort of source of moral and spiritual replenishment, in which and by which the family can restore its soul and enlarge itself.

It follows that in young maturity, just as we saw was true in adolescence, there is a way by which the iron grip of determinism of character can be broken. In speaking of the adolescent we were seeking to show that the individual self, although determined by the dynamic relationships out of which he came, is not fixed past changing. His life pattern can be remade in a new and higher dynamic relationship. And so it is now with the family pattern. In many instances a discernible family pattern comes down from previous generations; but it is not unchangeable, and if it is running down, that process is not irreversible. For a family as a group can be reborn, quite as truly as can the individual, and this is possible in a dynamic relationship between the family and a church which is capable of the function of enlargement.

THE CHURCH AND THE KINGDOM

The Kingdom of God is his kingship, or sovereignty, over man. The church and the Kingdom of God are not identical, but it is one of the functions of the church to be the scene where man is confronted by the claims of the Kingdom of God, that is, by God Himself and his moral demands as sovereign over human life.

We have sought to show throughout this book the remarkable cunning with which man contrives to avoid or to blunt the edge of those divine demands on the moral life. It is not merely that he forgets God or runs actively away from God, though he may indeed do both of these. But it cannot be too often emphasized that man has learned to be more subtle than the Elijahs and the Jonahs who sought a geographical escape. For we have discovered how to take the very weapons in the arsenal of religion itself, especially theology and even the church, and use them as shields to ward off the radical claims of God upon us men and our living.

Thus a degenerative process is always latent and often active in the church itself. And the corrective to this degenerative process is the Word of God in its two-fold form: Jesus Christ the living Word, and the Scripture as the written Word. So the church is, above all others, the place where the Word of God is allowed to confront man, speaking its own message undiluted and unscreened. The church can then become spokesman for God to those who know their own inadequacy, who desire the healing of the self down to its deepest foundations, and who are willing to face, not merely the word of man, but the Word of God, with whatever it may promise and whatever it may require.

This confronting of man by the living God who speaks through His Word, is at the core of the church's business in the world. It is the basis of moral leadership in a world of moral confusion and compromise. And young adulthood is a peculiarly strategic time for the undiluted moral demands of a holy God to confront the human soul, especially in the case of those who are mature enough to understand their meaning but not yet so deeply encrusted with convention that they dare not obey.

But only the poor in spirit can endure to face this ministry of the church. For this is not a ministry of comfort, but rather a ministry of high calling. It cannot be borne by the proud, for it would take away the root and ground of religious pride which is the most deadly form of pride; and it would leave the religionist naked of soul in the very house of God where he had taken shelter against God. But for those who come in poverty of spirit, knowing their need and being willing to be silent in order that God may speak, for them there is peace in God's acceptance as they are, and a readiness to take the next step of the pilgrimage toward what they might become or do.

CHAPTER FIVE

The Burning Bush

W E NOW HAVE in view a period of some two decades of middle life reaching, say, from about thirty to about fifty years of age. In the case of an individual, this period presents a mass of biographical detail with which we cannot here be concerned. And when larger numbers of persons are taken into account there is a wide range of differences between individuals, and we must pass by these also. For here, just as when dealing with the earlier periods of life, we are seeking for the central problem of character, which we may regard as common to all men, however divergent they may be in other respects.

It will be recalled that we have spoken of three central problems in the development of character in the earlier stages. These were, first, becoming an individual; second, becoming weaned from the parents; and third, making one's mature identifications and assuming his mature responsibilities. And now in an equally summary manner we may say that in middle life the central problem of a developing character is to achieve a mature view of life and the universe.

A VIEW OF LIFE

One's "view of life and the universe," as we use that term, is the *meaning* which he finds in all that has confronted him. It is what we often refer to as a man's "philosophy of life."

In this matter of a philosophy of life it is quite possible that we are dealing with an activity of the mind which is exactly as instinctual as growth itself. For the making of a philosophy of life is the self striving to relate, not to the parts, but to the whole. It is a striving to relate, not now merely to persons, or things, or to society and the flux of human events, or the world of adult life; but rather to the totality of all that has been, or is now, or ever shall be.

To speak in this fashion makes it sound as if a philosophy of life were a very complicated matter, requiring vast mental powers either to compose or to grasp. Not necessarily so at all. The most important philosophies of life have two great marks: they are profound, but they are simple. A philosophy of life which has any considerable significance is somewhat like a pass key. It can be seen in one glance. It can be accurately described in a few minutes. But put it to work, and the longer we use it the more doors we find it will open, until finally we find it gives us access to every part of the house.

The impulse to make a philosophy of life seems to be as old as self-conscious man, and certainly is a part of life as we know it today. Two examples, one from antiquity and one from our own time, will illustrate the point.

The first example may be taken out of Jewish life. It is said that every Jewish rabbi in ancient times was expected to sum up the wisdom of his entire life in one brief "saying," which he would teach to his disciples and which they would then treasure as the gist of what they had learned from him. A large number of these "sayings" have been preserved and make up the tractate known as *Aboth*, or *The Fathers*, which is in the Babylonian Talmud. This little book, then, contains a series of brief, pithy philosophies of life, each one the final garnering after years of mature reflection on the meaning of things.

The second example comes out of the observation of a modern university professor. Irwin Edman of Columbia, in his semi-autobiographical *Philosopher's Holiday*, has a chapter on "Philosophers without Portfolio." In this he relates story after story of persons whom he has known, outside of academic circles, who were seeking to reduce their philosophy of life to form. Some had achieved it, and could put their philosophy in a few crisp phrases. Others, more ambitious, were still struggling. Typical of the latter is the business man who spends a good part of his leisure trying to get a book written on a theme which he feels is vital, and then spends another generous share of time and of money as well in getting it published and circulated.

PHILOSOPHY AND CHARACTER

Now one certainly does not wait until middle age to begin forming his philosophy of life. As young man or woman, as youth, as child, even as infant, one is intuitively seeking the formula with which he can cope with life as life confronts him. The *formula* is the way, the pattern of character, which one actually uses in trying to cope with life. The *formulation* is the way he consciously explains his formula. His view of life, as already said, is the meaning he finds in all that confronts him, that is, in the totality of what he has been trying to cope with. His view of life, or his philosophy of life, if one prefers to call it that, is the interpretation which he gives to the whole of things in light of the formula he has developed as a way of dealing with a part of the whole.

It is useful, furthermore, to distinguish between a spontaneous philosophy of life and an acquired philosophy of life. A spontaneous philosophy of life springs out of one's own formulation and one's own formula for coping with life. An acquired philosophy of life, on the other hand, is one which we have been taught. It sprang in the first instance out of the formulations and formulas of other people, and it may or may not correspond with our own spontaneous philosophy.

It will be seen, then, that in considering a philosophy of life we have to reckon with at least four levels in the character structure. To take them in the order in which they might meet the eye as we come to know a person, they might be somewhat as follows:

The Acquired Philosophy

The meaning which one has been taught to give to life and the universe. This is something one is said to "hold," "profess," "support," "defend," and so on.

The Spontaneous Philosophy

The meaning we actually give to life and the universe as it confronts us, and as we deal with it day by day.

The Formulation

The way we explain ourselves to ourselves and others, at the level of conscious thought and of speech.

The Formula

The dynamic pattern of character which we actually use in striving to cope with life; largely a matter of feeling and emotion, and largely hidden from one's self-awareness.

Let us now illustrate briefly the kind of character material which the first three layers might contain in one individual, and the consequent reverberations in the fourth layer, that is, in his acquired philosophy of life. It must be understood of course that such an illustration as this is schematic and greatly oversimplified; and that the number of possible variations is very great.

In this illustration we start at the bottom. Let us suppose that the basic formula in some given person is aggression. He meets life by attacking it. He gets his way, or tries to, by shoving, dominating, threatening, using force, making people uncomfortable, putting them on the defensive, making them suffer, and so on. This has been his basic formula from a very early age.

As he tries to explain himself to himself and to others, his formulation may take any one of many possible shapes. Suppose, for example, that he can only understand himself by believing that people generally are aggressive toward *him*. The world as he feels it, then, is full of enemies, full of hate, full of danger. He feels there is abundant cause for suspicion and fear.

His spontaneous philosophy of life might conceivably take either one of two general directions. He might interpret the universe in terms that emphasize its unfriendliness, its danger to human interests and values, and so forth. If his philosophy of life is a religious one he may feel God as threat, jealousy, anger, wrath, and the like; and these may prove to be feelings of so deep-rooted a nature as to defy any reasoning which would lead to a different conclusion.

Or he might interpret his place in the world as one whose highest duty is to fight something; *what* he is to fight will vary and change with the passing of his years, but he must find something to fight. In a word, a flaw in his character has been canonized and has now become a virtue in his philosophy.

Then suppose, furthermore, that he has been subject to teaching and has acquired a religious philosophy of life which holds that mature love is essential to human well being. As that basic principle is elaborated into a "system," he can understand it intellectually, but not emotionally. His real God, it may be, will still be a God of wrath. And it is quite within the range of possibility that, professing a religious love, he will express that "love" by attacking men or doctrines or movements in the name of his religion. If he is a minister, he probably devotes much of his energy to working "against" this or that; he derives deep satisfaction from "taking a stand" on a matter; he is much given to denouncing evil, assuring us that he loves the sinner and hates only his sin; and he has much to say in praise of the prophet, the need for a prophetic ministry, and the like.

Now our especial concern in this chapter is not merely with a philosophy of life, but with achieving maturity in one's philosophy of life. We should, therefore, seek for factors that determine the degree of maturity which one achieves in his philosophy of life. Three of these may be especially called to attention, namely: the depth from which the basic formula springs, the integrity between one's spontaneous philosophy and his acquired philosophy, and the capacity for dealing with unanticipated reality. Let us examine these factors in that order.

DEPTH OF FORMULA

One way of evaluating the maturity of a philosophy of life is to determine the depth of the character problem which the basic formula of that philosophy is seeking to solve. In order to make clear what is meant by this statement, we must first recapitulate.

It will be recalled that in preceding chapters we have discussed the central problems of character which confront the human being in succession as he grows. The list of central character problems as we have presented it would look somewhat like this, if simplified to a schematic form:

> The Self, Establishing its relation with—
> Persons
> Things
> The Self or Ego
> Conscience or Self-judgment
> Personal role as masculine or feminine
> Role of parents
>
> ---
>
> Persons of same sex
> Authority
> Persons of opposite sex
> World of history
> World of adult responsibility

Now there are various basic formulas for dealing with the character problems encountered at each one of these levels. But as we have seen throughout the discussions, the formulas of the earlier years appear to influence or even determine the formulas of the later years of life. Accordingly in the above list we have drawn a line to indicate a rough distinction between more profound and less profound problems of character, and we now restrict our thought to the former, that is, to the more profound problems of character development. This leaves us with some six levels of the more profound problems of character, to which every human being must find his working solution.

In the next place, let us turn again now to the idea of basic formulas. It must now be recalled that the character problems encountered at any level will lead to the evolving of several typical basic formulas for meeting the problems of that level of growth. Each typical formula then can be expected to underlie a spontaneous philosophy which has been elaborated out of that formula. We would then have a group of philosophies clustering around each of the more profound levels of character growth.

Accordingly, if we take the six levels now under consideration, we may expect to find for each a group of philosophies of life especially concerned with the problems of character confronting the individual at that level of growth. This would yield us six groups of philosophies, which might be named as follows, beginning with the less profound and ending with the most profound:

> Philosophies of dependence
> Philosophies of role
> Philosophies of judgment
> Philosophies of the psyche
> Philosophies of materialism
> Philosophies of relationship

Before passing to brief illustrative examples of philosophies at each of these levels, two observations should be made: One is that when an individual evolves a formula and a philosophy at one of the less profound levels, he tends to seal himself off from solving his own problems of character at a more profound level unless his formula and his philosophy are shattered, and it does not necessarily follow that he will find a more profound philosophy then.

The other observation is that Christianity is not to be thought of as a neatly packaged philosophy of life which can be fitted into one and only one of these levels. Rather, in point of fact, Christianity is called upon by its adherents to support formulas and philosophies at every one of these levels. At each level, then, we shall usually find a secular formula and philosophy, and a Christian formula and philosophy. Then, in the case of a formula and a philosophy which Christians use, we still have to ask, "Is this the most profound, the most mature, formula of living and philosophy of life which Christianity is capable of yielding?"

We go on now to consider examples of philosophies of life at each of the six levels mentioned, beginning with the less profound and proceeding toward the most profound.

PHILOSOPHIES OF DEPENDENCE

At this level the formulas represent patterns of living as elaborated by persons who tend to have some or all of the following trends of character. They have not been able to free themselves well from dependency in their relation with parents or others. They are confused and perhaps terrified by the world of history which confronts them, and they seek a parent substitute on whom they can depend. In these cases the formulation has to be worked out in such a way as to preserve self-respect, while allowing dependency to continue.

Secular philosophies of dependence, elaborated out of such formulas, are illustrated by the political theory of the paternalistic state, the welfare state, and the like. Philosophies of this kind exert a powerful political appeal by such promises as work for all, security for all, and so on. This type of social or political philosophy helps a society which is losing its nerve to throw its burdens on a mythical father substitute called "The Government," thus preventing a more mature solution of human problems and yet at the same time preserving self-respect.

Religious philosophies of dependence rise and flourish under similar conditions, that is, in a world which is unstable, and surcharged with the feeling of imminent danger. And it appeals, similarly, to those who are frightened at the prospect of assuming adult responsibility in the moral and spiritual life.

Many branches of organized Christianity have built themselves up around some form of the philosophy of dependence as their core. This is true of course in Protestantism as well as in Catholicism. The symbols of expression vary but there is an underlying kinship at many points.

This is notably so in three respects. For one thing, the church takes on the role and even the name of "Our Mother." The minister becomes "Father," and the church or its doctrines or its head becomes infallible. Dependency on a spiritual parent substitute then becomes one of the most basic of all virtues.

The appeal of a religious philosophy of dependency is especially great when two conditions exist, namely, when a familiar culture is breaking up or when family life is deeply disrupted. Both conditions existed early in the history of Christianity when Catholicism was taking shape, and both conditions exist again now. It remains to be seen whether the Western world can keep its Christianity at the more mature level which it was beginning to know, or whether it will again predominantly take refuge in forms of Christianity based on philosophies of dependence.

Religious philosophies of dependence are frequently developed out of formulas somewhat different from those we have just been considering. In the development of character the individual may have failed to release himself satisfactorily from parental *authority*. In such cases the formula may prove to be one of continuing obedience and subservience to parental authority or one of continuing defiance of parental authority. The individual then evolves a formulation which will allow him to continue in adulthood either to obey or to defy early authority but which at the same time will help him to hide the identity of that authority from himself so that he can regard himself as mature, acting on his own convictions, and the like.

When a character problem of this kind is not well resolved it often results in a state of mind or a slant at any and all things, rather than in a particular philosophy. Thus, on the one hand, there is the mind which seems to approach any matter that arises with motives of obedience to authority which we readily recognize under such terms as conservatism, conformity, reactionism, fundamentalism, traditionalism and others with the same general meaning.

On the other hand, there is the mind which seems to approach any problem with motives of resentment against authority, rebellion against tradition and precedent. We are familiar with this pattern of response under such terms as liberalism, non-conformity, modernism, iconoclasm.

These two minds intuitively bristle at each other, and much controversy in religion is a conflict between opposites in character far more than it is a conflict between opposites in doctrine, although the latter may be real enough. For these patterns of character often reach the two contrasted stages which Moloney calls "neurotic conformism" and "neurotic non-conformism." [1] These two terms suggest the irrational dynamics operating in many controversies where something in religion is made to serve as a symbol around which the contestants can expend their neurotic feelings against each other for the supposed honor of God.

PHILOSOPHIES OF ROLE

It was previously pointed out that the individual takes his *character* role as masculine or feminine when quite young, and that his character role may or may not coincide with his *biological* role as male or female. It was further pointed out that one's relations both to persons of his own sex and to those of the opposite sex are deeply influenced by the solution to the problem of gender which he reaches while still very young. And now we have in view the situation of persons whose early solution of the problem of role as masculine or feminine keeps them in a continuing tension with themselves and society. Their basic formulas are the patterns of living which they have worked out as a way of meeting their own character problems.

The religious formulations and philosophies which touch the character problems of this area are many and complicated. Here we confine the attention to two. One of these may be called philosophies of rejection. The formulation takes various shapes, such as: fear of the opposite sex; regarding sex as low, or as temptation, Satanic, symbol of all that is forbidden.

Based upon formulations of this general kind, numerous customs or conventions have grown up in the church, expressing what we referred to as the philosophy of rejection. For example, monasticism, while a very complex phenomenon, is perfectly obviously a religiously governed congregating of men with men, and women with women. Celibacy is a rejection of marriage on the ground that certain "higher" spiritual duties could not be well carried out in the married state, and marriage is placed at a lower level of humbler piety. Again, according to an ancient custom and one which still survives in some quarters, men are seated in one part of the sanctuary, women in another part separated from them. Thus, viewing the long story as it has unfolded, it has proved possible for the individual who felt sex to be a psychic danger, or who felt marriage to be a psychic impossibility, to turn his character problem into the foundation of a spiritual edifice and, as it were, atone *by* his life for what he could not help *within* his life.

Again, there are philosophies of combat. Here the formula arises from the fact that the individual cannot fulfil his own role as masculine or feminine, and envies the role of the opposite sex, or feels it as a threat. The formulations then express antagonism between the sexes, in which one sex "fights for its rights," attacks or minimizes the rights and customs of the other sex.

The secular philosophies of combat between the sexes commonly are developed around a protest on the part of women against men. These have been identified at various times under such terms as feminism, woman's suffrage, woman's rights, and others, and the idea of crusade has been common. The mingling of religious and secular formulations in the case of an individual is not uncommon, as is well illustrated in Anna Howard Shaw's autobiography, *The Story of a Pioneer*. Religious philosophies of combat have typically been developed around a protest of man against woman, upholding man's position in a patriarchal form of society, interpreting "woman's place" as subordinate, developing a religious code for woman's dress, hair, customs.

PHILOSOPHIES OF JUDGMENT

Here the formulas represent patterns of living worked out by persons who are preoccupied with the moral evaluation of themselves. This takes in two contrasted types of character. On the one hand, there are the persons who can see little but evil in themselves, and who suffer from chronic self-condemnation. And, on the other hand, there are the persons who can see little or nothing but good in themselves and who suffer from chronic self-appreciation.

The first of these types is the more readily recognized of the two, because it has played so large a part both in religion and in psychology. Here the typical formulation has two core elements, somewhat as follows: "I am vile, evil, unworthy, guilty, a sinner. . . . God is offended, outraged at my sin, has turned His back, will not forgive."

The spontaneous philosophy which develops out of this formulation is commonly a religious philosophy. It tends to prolong the two elements just mentioned far out beyond the self and to see them as existing in the universe at large. Thus it readily takes the view that *all* men by inherent nature are as evil as the elaborator of the philosophy has felt himself to be in his blackest moments. And in the same way the character of God can be interpreted in terms which take one's hours of bitterest anguish and attribute the cause to God. The resulting religious philosophy can be expected to stress such doctrines as the complete depravity of all men, the heinousness of sin, and the justice and wrath of God.

In the character which spontaneously produces such formulations and philosophies, it is reasonable to believe that any or all of three things may be true. In the first place this *may* be an aftermath following upon some unsolved problem in parent-child relations, especially in one's relation with the father. Experience in counseling repeatedly reveals an early background of this sort; that is, the person who is carrying a crushing burden of self-condemnation often is a person who felt his father as a threat and could not relate to him deeply, warmly, and trustingly.

Some of our classic systems of theology appear to have some of their roots in the same kind of soil. Thus, for example, Augustine and Luther both underwent profound spiritual struggles in which the sense of sin is prominent. Both saw human nature in its natural state, in the darkest terms. Biographical information is far from complete, but at least it is suggestive. Augustine's closeness to his mother, and the reproaches to which he left his father exposed for all time, are familiar to every student of his life.[2] In Luther's case the harshness, or even the brutality, of both the mother and the father are to be observed; but with the passing of time the father's figure seems to stand out the more prominently of the two.[3]

In the second place, the individual conscience *may* have become the scene of an unconscious displacement of God. That is, the sufferer from chronic self-condemnation may in all sincerity believe that his conscience registers the judgment of an accusing God, when a better understanding of the dynamics of the self would show that it is not God who accuses him, but rather a hostile or threatening father who has become disguised as God.

And in the third place the self, although very religious in speech and activity, may be unable to attain peace until he can eradicate from his own soul all human sources of moral judgment upon him, and be related directly and solely to God. A large part of the spiritual struggle of Paul, Augustine, and Luther, for example, is the effort to do precisely this, and a vast company of others less known have been inspired to the same achievement in fellowship with them. But there are many, on the other hand, who have bogged down in a religiosity consisting of a religious self-condemnation endlessly prolonged. And by ceaselessly nurturing this one theme of self-reproach they unwittingly armor themselves against a deeper reconstruction of the self.

The contrasted type, who can see little or nothing but good in themselves and who remain in a chronic state of self-appreciation, is a familiar type in religious thought but it has not been well studied in psychology. Nevertheless it presents a problem in psychology quite as truly as it does in religion. For here the individual has passed a value judgment upon his own self which rather effectively prevents reconstruction of the character, when and if such change proves essential to fuller living.

Persons of this general type may have come to their present stage of character development along any one of several quite different roads. Only two of these need be mentioned here. The first is the case of those who have reacted strongly against the view that human nature is vile and have developed in its place the view that human nature is essentially good. Often, however, this attempt to solve the problem of self-evaluation by substituting one formulation for its opposite, fails to get at the deeper issues and leaves the self exposed more than before to *unconscious* self-condemnation. In this event it may be that neurotic symptoms will appear, diverting attention from the underlying problems in the structure of the character.

The other road is that of spontaneous self-admiration. In this case a person may have been arrested in character growth at a point where he had become a god to someone, such as a mother or a father. He was omnipotent in his own sight, as any child may be; but in this case perhaps he was allowed to continue to cherish this pleasant illusion. He was worshiped. He could do no wrong. His wish was law. Life has never shattered this spell for him. In his conscience, then, God is displaced by his own self. The adoring self passes judgment on the adored self, and finds it very, very good. And if he is a religious person, he takes this adoring judgment upon himself to be the authentic voice of God.

The philosophies that are built upon this formulation may be either secular or religious. Examples of the former are to be found in the numerous philosophies of life emanating from the Renaissance and the Enlightenment. Examples of the latter are the doctrines that go under the name of Pelagianism in the ancient church, and the "dignity of man" theologies and cults which flourished in New England during say, the first half of the nineteenth century.

In the philosophies, however, just as in the formulations, it is often difficult to distinguish between what is protest and what is spontaneous.

PHILOSOPHIES OF THE PSYCHE

The problems of this stage come from a level still deeper than those that underlie what we have called philosophies of dependence, of role, and of judgment. For we now have to reckon with the situation of those in whom the growth of the *consciousness of a self* has been arrested or distorted. They have not been able to find emotional security either in persons or in things; nor have they been able to make up for this lack by accepting some shallower form of security such as refuge in dependence or in role.

Their basic problem seems to be that they are not able to relate deeply to *any* person or object outside themselves, and at the same time are not able to relate satisfyingly even to themselves. And it appears that the basic reason why they cannot relate even to themselves is that the consciousness of self is fundamentally insecure. As one man put it in speaking of his own situation, "I did not have confidence in my own identity."

For when one is not able to relate in any direction outside of himself, the boundaries between the self and the not-self are blurred. The process of individuation is arrested or distorted. The "I" or "Ego" cannot then emerge into unshakably confident self-consciousness. Instead of an unbreakable unity, it may be that the Ego is a fragile thing, ready to fall apart at any rough touch from the world of reality. Then, as we say, there is "danger of going to pieces." Or, more terrifying still, the tiny self, trying to emerge from the matrix of the environing world into selfhood, feels itself being sucked down into the vortex of non-being, senses that it is about to be swallowed up like a solitary candle guttering in the midst of an abyss of darkness.

The most authentic formulations are to be found in those various forms of neurotic and psychotic behavior which exhibit either or both of two characteristics: the unity or even the very existence of the self is felt to be threatened; and the accompanying emotional state is variously described by such terms as dejection, melancholy, apprehension, despondency, depression, desperation, or despair.

Now when the unity, or the powers, or even the very existence of the self are felt to be in imminent danger, it often happens that the mental processes are quickened. The intelligence may work at "fever heat" to produce formulations which will explain the self to the self and attempt to determine the place of the self in the universe. Out of just such formulations have sprung many of the most notable formal philosophies. Indeed, much that wears the conventional label of "philosophy" is a re-examination of the nature, the powers, and the limits of the self and has been produced when the foundations of selfhood were felt to be in danger.

Among all the philosophies which bear some relation to threatened selfhood, two are of especial concern in the present connection. These may be called philosophies of despair and philosophies of omnipotence.

Spontaneous philosophies of despair have been produced in great abundance in modern times. The philosophies employ all possible vehicles of expression, such as, for example, fiction, poetry, drama, music, formal philosophy, and theology. One may discern at least two great waves of despair in modern times. One followed after the French Revolution had spent itself and the Napoleonic dream had collapsed.[4] The second began about the time of the First World War and is still upon us, arising out of global wars, depressions, the "cold war," the specter of atomic war, etc. And in both periods the philosophies of despair find expression both in secular and in religious terms.[5]

Out of this very abundant material, space will permit reference to only one example of a secular, and one of a religious, philosophy of despair in the early part of the nineteenth century. A secular philosophy of despair is exemplified in Schopenhauer's pessimism, a philosophy too well known to need more than a passing mention. But the personal situation out of which the philosophy sprang is significant. When Arthur Schopenhauer was about seventeen years old, his father died, perhaps by suicide, following an unhappy marriage. His mother then removed to Weimar where her manner of life outraged Arthur's sense of propriety and his loyalty to his father. She displayed open antagonism to her son, quarreling bitterly with him and, for the last twenty-four years of her life, not even seeing him. He never married, and was almost completely alone as far as mother, father, wife, child, or family were concerned; nor could he find refuge in the nationalistic fevers of his time.[6]

A religious philosophy of despair from this same general period is to be seen in the work of Soren Kierkegaard (1813–1855), a Danish philosopher whose work became something of a vogue when the present great wave of despair began to roll over men's hearts. His work as a whole is commonly classed in the school of philosophy known as existentialism; and existentialism has been defined from one point of view as a philosophy which tries to win certainty through despair; it incorporates the ordeal of suffering within its philosophical or theological structure.[7] Or in somewhat broader terms it might be said that existential thinking is thinking in which the present situation and the destiny of the individual thinker *are* the philosophy.

One of Kierkegaard's works treats specifically of despair, which is "the sickness unto death." And the connection between despair and threatened selfhood is suggested in the cryptic opening sentences of this treatise: [8]

> A. Despair is a sickness in the spirit, in the self, and so it may assume a triple form: in despair at not being conscious of having a self (despair improperly so called); in despair at not willing to be oneself; in despair at willing to be oneself.
>
> Man is spirit. But what is spirit? Spirit is the self. But what is the self? The self is a relation which relates itself to its own self, or it is that in the relation (which accounts for it) that the relation relates itself to its own self; the self is not the relation but (consists in the fact) that the relation relates itself to its own self. Man is a synthesis of the infinite and the finite, of the temporal and the eternal, of freedom and necessity, in short it is a synthesis. A synthesis is a relation between two factors. So regarded, man is not yet a self.

Beneath this existential philosophy of despair is a biography, not without its similarities to that of Schopenhauer. Much of the detail is wanting, but the broad outlines are reasonably clear. Soren's mother, who had been a servant in his father's household, became the latter's second wife five months before the birth of their first child. The boy, who was the seventh child of this marriage, seems to have "had no mother he could adore," and to have been unwholesomely close to the father. [9]

The father appears as a melancholy, self-accusing figure. The fear that his father's melancholia might descend to him also, haunted him. He was engaged to be married, but for reasons that are obscure could not go through with it. He took a university degree in theology but could not love the church nor feel himself deeply a part of it. He fell prey to what we would now call yellow journalism, was pilloried in the press and hooted on the streets by boys. [10] In short, this is the personal situation of one who undergoes what Kuhn has aptly called an "encounter with nothingness." [11] The result, looked at on one side, is the subjective experience of despair. Looked at on the other side, it is an existential philosophy, spontaneously elaborated *de profundis*.

What we have referred to as philosophies of omnipotence take their rise out of the same general kind of soil, that is, from threatened selfhood. But the reaction of despair is not allowed to have full play in consciousness; instead, and as a sort of garment with which to hide the despair, there is an inflation of the self to enormous proportions in its own eyes. It is the case of the pygmy who dreams he is a superman, wakes and believes his dream is true.

The philosophies spontaneously elaborated out of this formulation have played so large a part in modern times that the subject is still sore to the touch over much of the world. From among all the marks of this philosophy, briefly note four.

First, the element of revolt often is prominent, revolt against accepted conventions, morals, political forms, religion. This is known as Titanism—revolt against the reigning gods hurling defiance, and stirring up strife. Titanism is prominent, for example, in Machiavelli's "prince," in Nietzsche's "superman," in Karl Marx, Hitler, Mussolini, and many others who readily come to mind.

Second, superman cultivates the myth of his own omnipotence and invincibility, as, for example, with Napoleon and Hitler. In the third place, the superman, in his Titanism, often takes a course of action which drags him relentlessly toward a catastrophic but grandiose predicament which has no solution, and from which death, probably by self-destruction, is the only exit. This theme recurs in Wagner's operas, and appealed powerfully to Hitler.

And fourth, the biography of a superman often shows that beneath the myth of omnipotence lay selfhood which was threatened at some vital point, such as parental affection, masculinity, normality of body. The biographies of Napoleon, Nietzsche, Hitler and Mussolini will repay study with such factors as these in view.

PHILOSOPHIES OF MATERIALISM

At the still deeper level of character development to which we now turn, the formulas arise out of the situation where the individual, not being able to relate deeply to persons, has had to learn to relate deeply to things. Not having succeeded in finding his profoundest emotional security in persons and in human relationships, he has sought it in the physically objective. His formulations, then, must yield a plausible, rational basis to account for his preoccupation with things.

When the character development has been arrested at this stage, it is to be expected that the spontaneous philosophy as it emerges will find its center of gravity in the material world. The possible variations are almost unlimited, but a few classic lines of development stand out. Such a philosophy may, for example, concern itself with the theoretical aspects of matter, and may support the view that the ultimate reality of the universe is materialistic, consisting, say, of physical matter and physical processes; and it may contend that all phenomena of every kind are and must always be reducible to these terms. Or a philosophy of this kind may concern itself with the practical aspects of matter, particularly with its possession or its control.

In the practical philosophies of materialism the problem of possession has loomed steadily larger as modern civilization has developed. This problem has to do with the ownership and control of things—in such forms, for example, as land, money, natural resources, machines, tools, and the like. Among the philosophies which are preoccupied with the problem of possession, two great opposing trends are obvious. They may be called philosophies of collectivization, and philosophies of private ownership.

Now it is perfectly obvious that emotional security is being sought in the present time, in both these directions; that is, some seek the security in collectivism, others in individualism; but beneath this difference they have this is common: that all who are obsessed with the problem of possession are, as it were, being driven from within to seek emotional security in a relationship with things.

This being so it is more readily understood that each of these two is supported by both a secular and a religious philosophy; that is, there is a secular philosophy of collectivization, and a religious philosophy of collectivization; there is a secular philosophy of private ownership and a religious philosophy of private owner-ship. Thus religion in general, and theology and Biblical interpre-tation in particular, are courted by both sides in the present world struggle over possession.

In American Protestantism the dispute is bitter at the present time. Campaigns of propaganda and vilification are systematically conducted. The most effective smear just now is the single word "Communist," or "Capitalist," depending upon the point from which one stands ready to *besmirch* the name of one who is dis-trusted or disliked. But all these things, however important they may be in the total world of history, should never be allowed to obscure one crucial fact: both communism and the materialistic currents in Protestantism are building their case for human wel-fare and their campaign for world mastery at a level of secondary importance in the development of human character. That sec-ondary level is the level of things, rather than the primary level of persons.

And both the theoretical and the practical philosophies of ma-terialism are insidious as far as the growth and maturing of the self are concerned. For they represent a freezing of character de-velopment, as we have just said, at a secondary stage. Such a freez-ing of growth tends to block a more profound solution of the problems of character, and at the same time tends to render psychologically unnecessary those other solutions which are more superficial but in the long run perhaps less malignant.

If this much can be accepted as true, then it follows that in so far as Protestantanism allows itself to be diverted by the conflict between the philosophies of possession, it sells its birthright in the realm of relationships for a mess of pottage in the realm of things. But it hardly need be said that such a point of view does not give Protestants the right to disregard the physical needs of the underprivileged. Rather, it means that Protestants, when they are prepared to express the genius of their own type of Christianity, will seek to point the Gospel primarily toward relationships, and secondarily toward material goals.

To illustrate the point, consider the indictment of American life contained in that poignant but bitter autobiographical book *Black Boy* by Richard Wright. It takes only a few pages of this book to make one burn with shame in facing the physical degradation under which this boy had to grow up. That these conditions need remedy does not even admit of debate. But until Protestantism has a Gospel which will heal the human relations between the Negroes and the whites which permit such conditions to exist, it might be a more Christian thing to turn the religious mission in America over to some group of Christians who will seek *first* the Kingship of God over the relations between white and black. If that high goal were attained, "these things" would be added as within a family where love prevailed, without any need of a law to compel "fair practices."

PHILOSOPHIES OF RELATIONSHIP

The profoundest level from which character springs is the level of relationships between persons. The most dynamic of these ordinarily, as we have repeatedly said, are the earliest relationships between the individual and his parents. We have been seeking to show that if these earliest and most dynamic relationships are not favorable, the later unconscious formulas, the conscious formulations, and the philosophies which are elaborated will show the scars, and will seek to make up for the lack.

And now we come to the case of those whose earliest dynamic relationships *have* been favorable. In that event the basic formulas are likely to show that the individual can meet life with a maximum of adequacy and with a minimum of resort to those unconscious psychic stimulants or sedatives which we have been describing, such as seeking security in things, nurturing one's despair or his megalomania, living in endless self-condemnation or self-applause. One does not have to exhaust the repertoire of devices for supporting or protecting his own self-esteem. He is as nearly free to act and to think as one can ever expect to be. He can go straight to the heart of things, for he can deal with the roots of good and evil.

The philosophies which deal with relationships between persons are many in number. Here we shall only call attention to two types, which we may call the negative and the positive philosophies of relationship.

Negative philosophies of relationship, taken as a group, represent certain common characteristics; that is, they can be thought of as elaborated by persons whose character structures appear to have certain things in common. For one thing, they are persons who intuitively recognize that relationships between persons are primary in significance. But, second, their own personal experience in human relations has left them underprivileged as far as the giving and the receiving of the profoundest love is concerned. Life has not yielded them in experience the unmeasured security and satisfaction which they discern by intuition. And in the third place, within this contradiction between intuited possibility and experienced fact, they retreat from the closest human relations without necessarily abandoning those relations, and seek their security and their sufficiency within themselves. This is individualism, a sort of final resort for those who live within the midst of relatively normal human relations, thrive upon those relationships and praise them, and yet retreat from the emotional costs of the profound love which those relationships require of man.

The retreat leads in many possible directions and each one evidently tends to elaborate a philosophy to rationalize the retreat. As a single example, consider New England Transcendentalism. Prevailingly the creators of this philosophy appear in biography as people of high morals and exceptional intelligence, but poor in affect. Family life, where it exists at all, often appears in erratic, or frigid-sounding, or experimental forms. The idealized individual is self-reliant, self-sufficient. The profoundest relation, it would seem, is not to one's own flesh and blood but rather to some vague entity known as the "Oversoul."

The spiritual decay which followed hard on the heels of what Van Wyck Brooks has called "the flowering of New England," may well be regarded as an exhibit for Reinhold Niebuhr's thesis that the profoundest evil in human nature is pride. In this case the Tower of Babel would be the effort to create the Individual, a creature who can retreat from the deepest human relations, live in self-sufficient emotional isolation, and make poems to the Oversoul because one is beholden to no man and to no god.

Positive philosophies of relationship, on the other hand, reach the profoundest levels to which the human mind has as yet penetrated. For in the first place these philosophies build their case for human well being upon a primary level, the level of persons and personal relationships. This is the most profound level we know in the human scene because it corresponds to what we know of human growth, and thus brings creation and creativity into focus for the human mind to contemplate. And it is at the deepest level, further, because it refuses to be diverted into preoccupation with more superficial problems and more shallow-rooted solutions for the human predicament.

And in the second place these philosophies take what is known in human experience as the root of human well being, and use it as the best clue we have as to the constitution and functioning of the universe. Having known love in the human scene, they take that love to be not an accident, but rather to be a sample, a valid instance, of Something active in the universe, on a cosmic and eternal scale. To that Active Something the name of God is given. And then faith, as we sought to show in the first chapter, is the substance of the archetype; that is to say, faith means that we already experience the reality here and now.

The life, the teaching, the death, and the resurrection of Jesus Christ exemplify this philosophy as nothing else does. So much is this so that the Christian typically sees in this message and mission a revelation, a *Word*, from God. And this personal Word of God does not merely reveal a principle, as a philosophy might do. It does that, to be sure; but more than that by far, it reveals a way of healing, a way to "wholth" or wholeness, for those who have lacked love, and for those who have violated it. Such a revealing is no longer merely a philosophy of life. It is salvation to those who believe; that is to say, those who have faith are not merely giving credence to a set of philosophical propositions, but are taking hold of the "substance," the reality of the thing itself, and beginning to live by it and in it. And at last with more mature reflection one may come to understand that he is not merely grasping; he has been grasped by reality—reality from beyond himself.

INTEGRITY

Earlier in this chapter we suggested that three factors determine the degree of maturity of one's philosophy of life. One was the depth from which the basic formula springs, and we have just been examining that factor as we considered philosophies of dependence, of role, of judgment, of the psyche, of materialism, and of relationship. The second factor, we suggested, is the integrity between one's spontaneous and his acquired philosophies.

Complete integrity would exist if one's acquired philosophy coincided exactly with his spontaneous philosophy. In that event the view of the meaning of life which he has been taught is the same as the spontaneous view of life which springs from the depth of his own self. And in this case the acquired philosophy helps him to understand life as he, with his own particular structure of character, apprehends it.

On the other hand, integrity is impaired if one's acquired philosophy of life does not coincide with his spontaneous philosophy. In this case one has been taught a view of life which he "holds" intellectually, but this acquired philosophy is essentially alien to the actual character. Discrepancy between the philosophy of life which one has acquired and the formulation or philosophy upon which his life is really built, is one of the most obvious experiences of civilized man. The common attempt in middle life to work out one's own statement of his philosophy of life is an effort to get rid of the discrepancy between one's character and one's philosophy, and thus reach integrity. Where it exists in a given individual it may fairly be regarded as a sign of inward striving to achieve wholeness or unity within the self.

The quest for integrity may take the individual in the direction of a more profound philosophy of life, in contrast with a less profound one where he has hitherto rooted himself. The more profound view of life is also a more mature view of life. On the whole a movement in the direction of greater maturity and deeper foundations tends to be a regenerative type of experience, for one goes deeper down into reality in search of truth and security.

On the other hand, the quest for integrity between one's spontaneous and the acquired philosophies of life may take him in the direction of a *less* profound and *less* mature view of life. This kind of shift in the foundations of the self tends on the whole to be a degenerative type of experience, for one abandons the more profound basis of selfhood for the less profound.

We have been seeking to show that the profoundest and most mature view of life is the philosophy of positive relationship, that is, its unconscious formula, its conscious formulation and its articulate philosophy all are based on self-giving love, the "Agape" love of which the New Testament speaks, or the "mature love" to which modern psychiatry refers.

Now even as late as middle life a movement of the self toward integrity at this level is a regenerative experience, and a movement away from it is a degenerative one. Taking again the terms we have been using throughout this chapter, we might represent the thought in the following way:

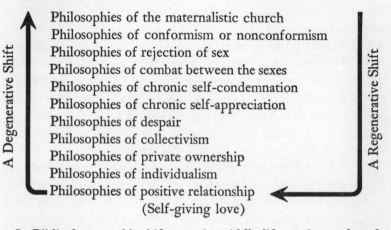

In Biblical terms this shift even in middle life to the profoundest foundations of being is variously referred to as "becoming as a little child," "returning to the mother's womb," "being born again when one is old," a "death and resurrection" of the self, and so on. It is an experience which maturing adults have sought in religion as far back as we have any knowledge of the history of religion. And Christianity offers the possibility that it can happen to anyone at any age.

THE BURNING BUSH

A third factor determining the degree of maturity in one's view of life is the individual's capacity to deal with unanticipated reality. This capacity is illustrated with remarkable symbolism in the account of Moses and the burning bush.[12] It is a story in which three things stand out as having especial interest for our present line of thought.

For one thing, it is the story of a man in middle life who had worked out his niche. He had his job to do, and everything indicates that by this time he had developed a philosophy of life which had sustained him through luxury, then through danger, and now held him together in the monotonous routine of a commonplace life.

But in the second place he was confronted by a fact which would not fit into his philosophy. To disregard the fact, rush past it, and protect his view of life from any further disturbance; or else to stop, look the thing squarely in the face, and if necessary let it take him into a deeper philosophy of life which could deal with this unanticipated reality: that was his choice, and he chose the latter.

Then third, and in consequence, he was invited to plumb a depth of reality which hitherto he had never known. Most significantly this deeper penetration into reality had to do with the nature of being, particularly the personal being of God: "I am that I am."

The possible parallel to the life of any man or woman in modern times hardly needs to be pointed out. The Burning Bush is our confrontation in middle life by some fact or condition or situation which does not fit our view of life. In the moment of that confrontation, one of the gravest temptations of middle life is upon us: whether to protect such peace of mind as our view of life yields us and hurry past the unanticipated Burning Bush; or else to cling to an inadequate view of life, trying to curtain off from sight and mind whatever will not fit it, counting the safety of even a poor harbor better than the perils of the open sea.

What is the Burning Bush? It may be any one of many things that will not fit the view of life which one has worked out by middle age. It is, for example, monotony when one had reckoned on a life filled with interesting experience, or it is catastrophe, sharp, crushing, terrifying, which befalls the beloved, or oneself, or falls across the wider landscape, or it is adversity when one had counted on comfort, or it is discovering to one's dismay that the self does not fit the role into which it has been drawn. Or it is discovering that God as He is does not fit the neat theology we had constructed.

In any and all such times the basic question which confronts us in the Burning Bush is this: is one ready as yet to know God as He is?

CHAPTER SIX

Into Thy Hands

WE ARE NOW TO CONSIDER the portion of life from about fifty years of age onward. The line which marks off middle life from old age is quite indistinct. It varies greatly as between different individuals, and even within the individual it is common now to distinguish many different kinds of age. For example, a person might be fifty years old chronologically. Biologically, however, he might be at a much greater age, with one or more organs of his body nearly worn out. But psychologically he might still be quite young in the sense that very little had ever happened to him. Emotionally he had never lived very far out into the stream of life.

Obviously these three kinds of age, chronological, biological, and psychological, could be found in every possible combination in one person. And still other kinds of age could be identified. But approaching the subject in that manner often leads to a rather fruitless discussion of the time when one is to be called "old." Let us simply say that we have in view the situation of those who have reached or passed the milestone of half a century. And it seems more frank to refer to them simply as "the old," or as "older people."

SIMPLIFICATION

In each of the earlier periods which we have considered we have sought to identify the central problem of character development. Thus we have discussed individuation, weaning from parents, establishing basic identifications, and achieving a mature view of life as being central problems of character in childhood, youth, young maturity, and middle life, respectively. And now after the same fashion we may say that the central problem of character in age is simplification. In Chapter I we spoke of the final stage in human development as "achieving simplification of life in its physical, material, and spiritual aspects, so that the soul may with less and less impediment progress toward its chosen destiny."

By the term "simplification of life" we mean distinguishing the more important from the less important, getting rid of the less important or relegating it to the margin; and elevating the more important to the focus of feeling, thought, and action. The standard by which the individual distinguishes between "more important" and "less important" is contained within his philosophy of life, especially in his spontaneous as compared with his acquired philosophy.

This being so, simplification of life in old age can be expected to be thorough-going or superficial, depending upon the level at which the person's view of life had been worked out in his earlier years. Thus, for example, if by middle age one's view of life consisted essentially of a materialistic philosophy, as we used that term in the preceding chapter, then in old age it can be expected that the individual will contrive some way to elevate *things* into a sort of final sacramental act at the close of his life. We shall further illustrate the point later in this chapter.

It is to be borne in mind that a final simplification of life at a more profound level than one has lived in throughout his earlier years, is quite within the range of possibility at any point during these final decades. Indeed, in some societies, as in the Far East, it is an accepted thing that one should radically simplify his life in the direction of spiritual values in his latter years. And in Western culture some persons do essentially the same thing. But the inertia of habit is great, and until very recently it was something of a western folk ideal that a man should "die in harness," or "die with his boots on."

That is to say, one hoped to drive himself in the old familiar direction until death overtook him and he "dropped in his tracks."

But it may well be true that this folk ideal of the West is changing under our very eyes, and that the world of history as it unfolds is confronting the old with a few more years of life and, for the first time, a little decent leisure, in which to simplify life in its closing stage.

What is meant will perhaps become more apparent as we consider certain aspects of life as the old now encounter them in the modern world.

A NEW CONTINENT

The old now are beginning to constitute a sort of new continent in the modern Western world of population. This is true as to their life expectancy, their number and proportion in the population, and their role in society.

As to expectancy, the median or "average" age in the United States has been rising steadily for a century and a half and is expected to continue to rise. In 1800 the median age was approximately sixteen years. In 1900 it was about twenty-three years; in 1945 about 29.7 years, and the Bureau of the Census estimates that in 1975 it will be about 34.1. Both the number and proportion of people sixty-five years of age and older in the United States are increasing. In 1870 there were a little over a million, in 1900 there were about three million and in 1945 there were about 10 million. It is forecast that the number will be well beyond 17 million in 1975.[1]

The proportion as well as the absolute number is increasing, and a 45 to 55 per cent increase in the proportion of the population sixty-five years and above is expected in the period 1945 to 1975.

The new place coming to be held by older people in modern society is shown in too many ways to permit even mentioning all of them here. But socially, politically, and economically they constitute a new force to be reckoned with, and in many respects a new problem to be solved.

To science they have yielded a new field of inquiry, called gerontology, or the study of aging. In medicine they have required a new field of specialization called geriatrics, or the care and cure of the aged. In organized religion they have confronted the churches with the question of how their needs may best be served by pastors and congregations.

Now this new continent of population might be examined from many points of view, as is quite fittingly being done in current discussions, projects, and writings. But in this connection we wish to make only two points stand out: the first is that the world of history is presenting to individual man a few more years of life and leisure; and second, this prolonged final span tends to be a blessed gift if one can make it a time of radical simplification at a profound level of ripe maturity. Otherwise the prolonging of years tends to mean little but an extension of "labor and sorrow," and as such is a dubious gift at best.

Let us then examine a few of the areas in which character is newly tested during the later decades of life, and in which growth of character by simplification is needed. And in doing this we shall seek to keep one point of view throughout, namely, that the present trend toward longer life makes continued character growth the more imperative if modern Western civilization is to profit morally and spiritually by the opening up of this new continent of human life.

SIMPLIFICATION OF STATUS

One of the more obvious sets of changes overtaking one as age advances is change of status, and that in several respects.

For one thing, the individual changes status in the complex web of family relationships. Of course he remains a father, a mother, a sister, a brother, or whatever else he may have been in a family group. But the *meaning* of his role changes in the sense that seed has become fruit.

Love, kindliness, consideration, poured out into human relations in the twenties, the thirties, and the forties, now begin to bear such a harvest as they could not bear much earlier, for one now begins to move into old age loved, respected, trusted, even venerated. But, on the other hand, if one has invested his relations to the members of his family with selfishness, with distrust and suspicion, or with rejection and hatred, then the bitter bread he has cast on the waters comes back to him more bitter still. And as he moves on toward the end he is borne up by the bonds of a steadily strengthening love, or else he begins to feel himself deserted and lonely long before he has lived out his years.

Peculiarly difficult is the case of the solitary survivor of a family. If he has invested little emotionally as the years passed, he is perhaps not much more alone when solitary than when surrounded by relatives. But for one who has loved deeply and been loved devotedly, but who is now the last remaining leaf on his tree, there is a pathos too deep for expression and a need which, if it be not met spiritually, can hardly be met at all.

Again, one's economic status is likely to change in one or many ways after about middle life. Due to the premium placed on youth in a competitive and industrial civilization, the average earner probably begins to feel economically insecure, say, at least as early as forty-five. And if he keeps his job until around sixty-five, he is likely to be compulsorily retired. In any event one tends to become economically dependent in some sense as age advances. If there is some form of old-age pension or other income, the person preserves a type of self-respect which is highly significant in the character structure of old age. If he does not have this resource, his sense of dependency or even of poverty creates a strain which some of the aged endure with dignity, while others frankly become askers even to the point of open beggary.

Yet again, status tends to change in respect of prestige. As family status changes and as one gives up his job, prestige may dwindle too. He then will typically accept the altered prestige with such grace as he can muster, or devise ways to prop and bolster his waning prestige.

Now these changes in status in family, in economic position, and in one's prestige value are severe tests of one's character as age advances. And one is obliged to ask whether, in Western civilization, men as a whole can stand up to these tests as well as women do. In so far as the answer is favorable to women, the implication for men would seem to be this: that men tend to need more relearning of life from middle age onward than women do. It is a well-known fact that women tend to live to an older age than men. Could it be that one of the reasons lies in this general area?

In any event if one's *essential* status in personal relationships has been sound, then as age advances he can slough off the temporary aspects of the role he has been obliged to play without disturbing too greatly the core of his selfhood. The more casual and superficial changes of status which come with the passing of years bring no profound disturbances, and one can move into old age, not with panic, but with serenity.

PHYSICAL SIMPLIFICATION

By "physical simplification" we have in mind what tends to happen in the body in old age. In general, *what* the body can do is dwindling until eventually the capacity for physical functioning is completely lost, at which time physical death ensues. But each diminution of capacity is a threat to the self, and character is both tested and made manifest by the manner in which the fact of dwindling capacity is met.

The body ordinarily begins its waning long before we think of an individual as being old. The turn from the waxing body to the waning body begins very early, perhaps typically in the twenties, but the decline is ordinarily so slow as to attract little or no attention. But with the passing of the decades the body begins to flash its unmistakable signals to warn one that the body has started its long path of decline which leads now toward a setting sun.

In Western life when an individual receives his first signals of approaching age, one of the major tests of character is upon him: to reject and deny it, or to accept and affirm it. Shall one try frantically to freeze his life processes at some such age as thirty or less which he fancies he will never pass? Or is he able to be his age and move on with the profound life current which bears him forward to deeper seas and eventually wider harbors? With such general alternatives before him, one is put to the test in many respects day after day, as the years move on.

For example, there is the need to simplify work, for the obvious reason that capacity for work is waning. Around this problem for character growth, whirls a vast pother and to-do in American life, people pretending they are "as good as I ever was," being mortally offended at the mention of gray hair, or shortened breath, or wrinkled skin. It is a species of indecent exposure of the naked self, terrified at the prospect of aging, which the world of nature thrusts upon us but which a competitive civilization refuses to accept and honor. Here once more the soul, if it would avoid being crushed, must simplify itself in order to get above the Juggernaut.

Again there is the character test which waning sexual capacity thrusts upon one with the advent of middle life and old age. Here, as in all else with which we are dealing, the basic structure of the character determines how this particular bodily change can be handled. In so far as an individual life is oriented around sex as a physical function and a sensual experience, to begin to lose it is a source of dismay or even of panic.

But on the contrary, when sex is contained within a web of profoundly satisfying human relations, then both the waxing and the waning of sexual capacity can be accepted as phases in the cycle of personal creativity. In that event love contains sex, but is vastly deeper, wider, and longer than sex. Sex is of time, and gradually subsides. Love is eternal, rejoicing in the body of the beloved, yet not decaying with the decay of the body, nor dying with its physical death. Love "abideth."

Once more, in old age one has commonly to reckon with disabilities, malfunctioning of this or that part of the body, or helplessness whether partial or complete. Often these impairments gravely disturb the equilibrium which the self has worked out up to the time of the onset. The disturbance to the family many times is even greater since their routine of life is upset, the budget is thrown out of balance; and mounting resentments cannot be openly expressed, neither can they be successfully concealed. In all this the aging person carries the old self into the new situation and meets it by his own basic formula, whatever that may be.

Yet it is true that in many instances the aging person in his suffering achieves a triumph of character in the closing years, and out of the stuff of his personal tragedy weaves a parting gift to life which surpasses in value all that he had ever wrought before. This, many times, is an aged person's final discovery of the meaning of the Cross, namely, that out of *present* suffering as well as out of that which took place long ago, there may come a redemptive gift which is the gift of the suffering yet triumphant self. This discovery he translates into the speech of his contemporaries through the language of his own meeting of pain. They, hearing it, knowing it to be an authentic translation and purged at last of human dross, thank God and take courage. To discover these things is not to plumb the depths of cosmic meaning which broke forth on that Hill, but at least it is truly to know "the fellowship of his suffering," that is, to share the Cross at last in very fact.

MATERIAL SIMPLIFICATION

The term "material simplification" refers to the way one deals with *things* in the closing epoch of his life. As we pointed out in a previous chapter, the individual while still an infant encountered the world of things and established his basic formula in relation to things. In the most general terms it can be said that he learned to make things either secondary or primary. And now as age overtakes him the final consequences of his earlier relationship to things are lived out.

We can readily distinguish two broad types of material simplification as worked out by older people. The first is employed by persons who have found their basic emotional security in the world of persons and personal relationships, more than in the world of things. The typical pattern of material simplification in such a case consists in relegating *things* further and further out toward the margin of selfhood as age advances. For the sake of convenience let us call this the pattern of relegation of things, or simply "the pattern of relegation." Its conscious formulation is well expressed in the proverbial saying, "We brought nothing into this world, and it is certain we can carry nothing out." [2] That is to say, such a person intuitively understands that for him selfhood is not essentially dependent on things.

In actual living this pattern of relegation makes itself evident in any of many possible ways. For one thing there is a shrinking field of things upon which one feels dependent and without which he feels deprived and restless. This is often symbolized by the house or the room occupied by an aged person who once lived in more ample quarters. If the pattern of relegation comes natural to him, the place is not cluttered like a refugee's cart, with everything he could bring with him. Instead he has been able to give a hard and healthy pruning to the material extensions of the self; and now, even though his things have shrunken to what a single small room can hold, the place seems spacious, not cluttered but, as it were, open and roomy for the aging self still to grow in.

Again, in the pattern of relegation the individual can dispose of his things in such a manner as to fulfil two prime requisites of genuine giving. In the first place, the giver is not inwardly compelled to feed his own ego by the act of giving; therefore he can keep himself in the background and he does not need to fan up his own glory by seeing to it that his name is always kept to the front wherever his gift is used.

And in the second place in disposing of his things, whether money, land, or whatever, he can take his hands off the gift and permit the beneficiary to be, not merely an executor to carry out an order, but a true recipient who is permitted to use his judgment in using the gift. He does not feel compelled to give in such a way as to perpetuate his own power and his own will after his death. Both these marks of genuine giving are constantly being exemplified by older people who either dispose of part or all of their belongings while still living or else through their wills direct what disposition is to be made of their possessions. A very large part of the educational, scientific, charitable, and religious work of the Western democracies is carried forward by means of gifts made in this spirit.

Then, on the other hand, there is a second broad type of material simplification, worked out by persons who have found their basic emotional security in the world of things. In this case the typical pattern of material simplification can be called the pattern of concentration.

For as life draws toward its end the self in this instance seems to identify more and more deeply with its things until the self, as it were, is finally concentrated into, and absorbed by, its possessions.

Here the tendency is to surround oneself with things of some kind, upon which one is so dependent that he cannot part with them. The "things" may be any kind of objects which one cares to mention—money, securities, furniture, works of art, or junk. But the objects form as it were the outer skin of the individual, the surface which the self presents to the world.

There are socially approved forms by which the pattern of concentration may express itself, as in "wealth" of some sort which one devotes a life to amassing and from which he cannot bring himself to part. And there are forms which are counted "eccentric" because what is hoarded by the individual is not commonly given the same high value by society. But the psychological drive to surround oneself with a barricade of things is perhaps the same in either case, and it can be appreciated better if seen in its more naked form.

For example, there is a type of story which appears in the newspapers again and again, which has this theme beneath the variant details: "Aged recluse is found dead in his house, surrounded by the accumulated debris of a lifetime. He was well off, but he spent next to nothing, threw nothing away, lived like a pauper, and died alone."

In one recent story of this pattern an aged woman's hoard was found to contain diamonds to the weight of a thousand carats, and a number of checks, held so long they could not be cashed. In another, two aged sisters lived in seclusion. They had owned two houses, but had been living on relief. Their apartment was stacked high with old newspapers, cardboard cartons, books, old magazines, and the odds and ends of two lifetimes. The doors were blocked, and narrow paths were left open between walls of junk. When the police entered, one sister was lying on the floor beneath a littered bed, dead, the body being gnawed by rats; while the other sister was sitting in a little cleared spot in the kitchen, babbling incoherently.

Further, in the pattern of concentration the individual, if he is able to dispose of his things, seems impelled to do so in a way which will exalt his own ego, and prolong his own will and power after his death. Here we have the frequent spectacle of the aging individual who gives, but contrives conditions which, as he hopes, will keep his name and fame alive, and which will permit him to keep his hand on the gift and its users, if possible, to the end of time.

A rather dramatic instance was reported recently. An aged man who had never married had amassed a fortune amounting to a huge sum. He sought to give it to some educational institution which would pledge itself to teaching a certain political doctrine as to states' rights, and a certain social doctrine as to race relations. At the last account he had not been able to find any school ready to bind itself in such a way that this aged man's will for his race and his nation could be propagandized into the life of the young for all generations to come.

SIMPLIFICATION OF CHARACTER

As simplification of status, of body, and of possessions takes place it becomes more apparent that these are merely aspects of a still deeper simplification which is going on. This we may call the simplification of character. That is to say, the basic formula by which one has met life in his earlier years often tends in his later years to stand out with still greater clarity. Disguises and pretenses drop away, and the self is more and more stripped bare, to be seen for what it really is.

It will be recalled that in the preceding chapter we spoke of spontaneous philosophies of life, especially those which we called philosophies of dependence, of role, of judgment, of the psyche, of materialism, and of relationship, respectively. We also spoke of the basic formulas, or basic patterns of character structure and motivation, underlying each of these. And now as we think of simplification of character in old age, it is possible to think of the individual's simplification as tending to take place at or near one of these levels.

However, the basic formulas underlying three of these often exhaust themselves or exhaust the individual before old age. Thus persons whose basic formula had to do with his gender role may find that this motive has exhausted itself by the later decades of life. In that event they may continue the earlier role by the inertia of lifelong habits; or the character may move toward a different basic formula and hence a different view of life.

Persons whose basic formula had to do with profoundly threatened selfhood, and whose view of life was chiefly compounded of despair, often die long before old age, or else, if they survive, may be psychotic. And persons whose basic formula was some type of severe self-condemnation or extreme self-appreciation, if they cannot find a more adequate basis from which to meet life, very often end life in a psychotic state of excessive self-condemnation and depression, or at the opposite pole, in exalted delusions of grandeur.

This leaves basic character patterns of dependence, of materialism, and of relationship, respectively, as types of basic formulas common in old age. Any one of these may furnish a basis of survival into old age. We have already spoken of some frequent typical outcomes in old age when the basic formula of the individual life was one in which emotional security was sought in things.

The simplification of character in old age around one of these three general types of basic formulas, viz., dependence, things, or personal relations, is very well illustrated in a study reported by Maves and Cedarleaf.[3] Their classification is somewhat different from our own, but their results, we suggest, bear a rather close resemblance to what we have just been saying. They studied the character patterns of seventy persons sixty-one to ninety-five years of age who were well known in the pastoral relationship. They distinguished three general patterns of character in these older people, called, respectively, persons who in old age were successfully creative, those who were still struggling toward creativity, and those whose creativity was submerged. The descriptions they give are of value.

Of the seventy aged people, they considered eighteen to be "successfully creative." They were thus described:

A. They had consolidated the basic trends of their entire life experience into a pattern which, while in earlier life it may have appeared less plainly, had now emerged as positive.

B. They had made and inwardly accepted a meaningful, and to them rewarding, readjustment to the specific losses of later maturity.

C. They had discovered and utilized what were for them the relevant compensatory and creative satisfactions which are possible to later maturity.

D. They had developed a unity and integrity in the organization of their psychic lives, which usually meant a considerable degree of inner peace and serenity.

E. They were basically creative and productive in their relationship to themselves, to other people, and to God.

F. They tended to be able to handle any but the most overwhelming threats or demands for readjustment which arose in their present experience, within their basic pattern of personality.

Maves and Cedarleaf regarded twenty-four of the seventy as being persons "struggling toward creativity," who are described in these terms:

A. Although suffering from inner conflicts they had nevertheless not inwardly given up hope of becoming successfully creative.

B. While they were restless and had found very little peace of mind, they had nevertheless not been able to seek an illusory serenity by submerging their potential creativity.

C. While they had apparently adjusted effectively to certain of the inevitable losses of later maturity, they had not inwardly accepted those losses in such a way as to be able to move on to the new types of potential satisfaction and creativity.

D. Although they had not organized their life purposes around destructive goals, neither had they yet been able to focus them around the creative vision of life of which they had somewhere in their experience had an inkling.

E. Although their energies were diffused and were used in a disorganized fashion, they had not tried to solve the difficulty by suppressing the energies.

F. Although any new threat or demand or frustration in the present situation induced anxiety in them, they were often capable with help of using such crises to move in the direction of successful creativity.

Further, they considered twenty-eight of the seventy to be individuals in whom creativity had been submerged. These persons are characterized in this manner:

A. Having found life in fact very difficult and frustrating, they had reacted by suppressing the creativity itself.
B. They had felt so insecure about dealing with the "war in their members" that they had moved away from the battle lines of life.
C. They had consolidated uncreative patterns which had all along been most fundamental though previously less apparent. In various ways they had attempted to deal with the losses of later maturity by not accepting them.
D. They had developed little capacity for mutuality in relationship to other people, for tolerance and acceptance in relation to themselves, or for true humility in relation to God. There was little or no capacity for give and take in their lives.
E. Because they could not accept the reality of their losses they had been unable to utilize any of the compensatory satisfactions or potentialities of later maturity.
F. When confronted with any frustration or new demand they tended to react in terms of the uncreative and blind main pattern, whether it was withdrawal, resentment, self-accusation, exaggerated activity, or something else.[4]

In the material just quoted it is further to be noted that these workers found the struggle to grow continuing right on into old age. A few were not only definitely defeated but had accepted defeat. But many, not only in the second group but in the third or "submerged" group also, were still struggling at this advanced age to achieve a simplification of character at a more creative and a more satisfying level.

In the terminology which we have been using throughout this book the most profound level at which character can be simplified is that of persons and personal relationships. The most profound of the relationships is the positive one—mature, outgoing love. When the character simplifies at that level as age advances, the sloughing off of the superficial and the casual components of the self leaves as it were a white, pure core which is essentially at home anywhere in the world with all sorts and conditions of persons; and at the same time it already feels at home in eternity since the self already knows its way in the midst of eternal values.

SPIRITUAL SIMPLIFICATION

It is to be expected that one's philosophy of life will also simplify still further in old age, unless it has already reached great simplicity at an earlier stage.

If the individual has developed a secular, to the exclusion of a religious, view of life, he will sometimes be found struggling against religious concepts and values until the very end of his days. It is as if he were still trying to persuade himself there is nothing to religion, and never quite succeeds in convincing himself. Or, and perhaps more frequently, he settles into what has been called "practical unbelief," that is, a course of life in which religious values play no conscious part at all. From a wholly secular perspective the tale of the years is told out to the end. In this case the end is taken by the individual to be truly the *end* of all, for him as a person. There may be a little talk of immortality through one's descendants, or the immortality of influence; or we are quite as likely to overhear this person saying that "one world has been enough," or he has "no desire to live forever," or "the wish for immortality is a selfish wish," and the like.

But regardless of the particular negative view of immortality which may be held, we are speaking now of the individual whose practical view is that human life is bounded by time, by nature, and by our planet, and bound in such a manner that to die is the end of all that we have known ourselves to be. The saga has sung itself out, and when the echo, too, dies away, that will be all. There is no more.

On the other hand, if one has developed a religious view of life, we can expect that the religious outlook will simplify at the level of one's own spontaneous philosophy of life. At the same time, however, we must be prepared for the possibility that even in old age the spiritual outlook will not only grow simpler and clearer, but also grow more profound.

Among all the kinds of spiritual simplification which actually take place, two processes seem to be going on. It should be emphasized, however, that these do not necessarily wait until old age. One is a decreasing interest in those religious values which the individual finds to be marginal in his religious philosophy. This is the negative side of spiritual simplification. It means definitely getting rid of some things in the spiritual life which one has tried to carry, out of a sense of duty, but which he has found are only a burden. And it means pushing other things in the spiritual life so far out to the margin that they will never again impede his spiritual growth.

It would seem that this negative simplification is especially necessary in the case of persons who have had careful religious instruction from parents or church. For such a person often, perhaps normally, finds that he must put off some of the cargo which loving, conscientious hands put upon him. It is not necessarily a question of whether the teachings which he feels he must abandon are true; perhaps the teaching which one feels compelled to abandon contains truth of greater absolute value than the teaching which he keeps and makes central. It is, rather, a question of the teachings which one finds to have no functional value *to him*. In other words, it is a prolonging of the quest for integrity between one's spontaneous and his acquired religious philosophy of life.

Instances of the negative side of simplification are, of course, very abundant. No doubt they are to be seen in the life of any person who has continued to grow spiritually in middle life and in old age. A few examples will be sufficient to illustrate.

There may be a simplification of *doctrines*. In this case a person who once had been absorbed in the minute details of an elaborate system of doctrine, finds himself sorting his beliefs into some order of relative importance, cherishing some and neglecting the others.

This is sometimes the case with men whose early religious interest was apologetic, that is, a "defense of the faith." One such person expressed the change which had overtaken him as he grew spiritually, by saying, "I used to try to garrison the whole frontier of Christian doctrine; but now I find I had much better garrison my own heart."

Simplification may take place in the realm of Christian duty. One may have been exceedingly zealous for this or that activity which he considered it his duty to follow, only to discover as time passes that this particular "duty" is taking him away from God rather than toward Him. A certain American minister, for example, in his early professional life distinguished himself by his aggressive prosecution of men whom he considered heretical. In later life, however, he became mellow with kindness and virtually disavowed his earlier career.

Or simplification may concern itself with the practices of worship. For as one comes to see worship more and more as a direct and unmediated transaction between the soul and God, some of the outward forms seem to matter less and less. Thus in the writings of Roman Catholic mystics one often senses that the soul has risen above the sacrament of the mass, and now knows how to commune with God and partake of Him face to face, without physical aids. Similarly with many mature Protestant Christians as they grow old; they miss the comradeship of fellow Christians joining together in the acts of worship, but they no longer *require* the aid of man in meeting God.

On the positive side, spiritual simplification is focusing upon the center in the total field of spiritual values, and doing whatever is possible to keep that center clear, warm, and active. The form which this positive simplification takes will vary with individuals, of course, but a few instances will illustrate what happens.

According to an ancient tradition,[5] the Apostle John became Bishop of Ephesus and labored there until, at a great age, he grew too weak to preach or even to stand. They would carry him to the church, seated, and he would say one sentence to the assembled people: "Little children, love one another." That was his entire life teaching concentrated into one sentence.

As Phillips Brooks drew toward the end of his ministry in Boston, after a long life, his biographer tells us that one theme began to dominate all that Brooks said to his people. That was the theme of God's fatherhood and man's sonship. Again and again it would be put in such manner as this: "God is your father. Be to Him as a son. Thus you will know the fulness of life." [6]

Or the spiritual simplification is often made evident by that in the Scriptures which the individual makes central. Thus John A. Hutton, editor of the *British Weekly*, proposed that Paul's message to the world was summed up in the passage, "Finally, brethren, whatsoever things are true, whatsoever things are honest, whatsoever things are just, whatsoever things are pure, whatsoever things are lovely, whatsoever things are of good report; if there be any virtue, and if there be any praise, think on these things. Those things, which ye have both learned, and received, and heard, and seen in me, do: and the God of peace shall be with you." [7]

Whether or not this is the deepest insight into Paul does not, for the moment, matter. But it *does* tell us what was central to Hutton. Professor Wayne Oates proposes that the portions of the Bible which a disturbed person uses in his stream of thought and speech provide a valuable clue to the nature of his problem.[8] There seems to be no inherent reason why the same principle should not apply in the case of emotionally healthy and mature persons also; that is, what they seize upon as the core of the Biblical revelation suggests the structure of the core of the simplifying self. This is the burning arc at which the Word of God and the soul of man have met. It is the "single eye" of which Jesus speaks, giving light to all the rest of one's personality house.

When the self is simplifying positively at the profoundest level, which is the level of persons and personal relationships, this means that the aging but still growing person is increasingly basing all his selfhood on *love*, outgoing and mature love in the New Testament sense of Agape. Love then toward God and man becomes more and more the very core of the simplifying self when the spiritual simplification is going on at this profoundest level.

In the Pauline conception of this kind of spiritual simplification love becomes the "bond of perfectness." That is, love is the girdle or ligament which holds all the other strands of character in place. When the character structure is of this kind, the personality as a whole can move on and grow on toward its goal of "perfectness," that is, the completeness or wholeness toward which its own inner nature is impelling it. The picture is a striking one:

Put on therefore, as God's elect, holy and beloved, a heart of compassion, kindness, humility, meekness, long-suffering; forebearing one another, and forgiving each other, if any man have a complaint against any; even as the Lord forgave you, so also do ye: and above all these things put on love, which is the bond of perfectness. And let the peace of Christ rule in your hearts, to the which also ye were called in one body.[9]

THE CHURCH

Thus far we have said little as to the losses which are almost certain to overtake older people, that is the personal losses which are suffered by the scattering of families and especially by the death of the best beloved. There is a real sense in which nothing in the human scene can ever compensate for the loneliness which follows.

On the face of the matter it seems that human tragedy is only deepened if one bases his whole life on love, and then loses the beloved. And that *is* the case if there is no sustaining fellowship of persons in the midst of whom the loss can be borne, and if there is no reasonable hope of personal reunion with the beloved. But it is precisely those two conditions which Christianity meets and thus draws the worst fangs of aging loneliness.

The first condition, that of a sustaining fellowship within which loss and loneliness can be borne, is the Christian church. The church is, itself, a larger family, not to replace the intimate ties of the household, but to provide a continuity of unbroken human fellowship within which growth toward completeness can be going on whether by households or by the solitary survivor of a household.

One of the church's greatest services to older people lies just here. Personal observation and careful studies unite in stressing the significance of the supporting human fellowships within which the aging can move on toward their sunset. Church "activities" and programs seem commonly to play a decreasing part as age advances, but the warmth of a simple, genuine affection from pastor and congregation is truly a bread of life and a water of life to the old, and especially to the bereft and lonely.

The other condition, namely that of a reasonable hope of reunion with the beloved, is met by the Christian hope of resurrection and immortality. Let it be called hope rather than a demonstrable proposition. But let it also be called a *reasonable* hope; for, as we pointed out in our opening chapter, *faith is the substance*, that is, the present experiencing of the reality, of everlasting life.

And if Christianity is a daring venture in one's relation to all that exists, as indeed it is, the quality of daring in one's venture of faith does not lie so much in his daring to *hope* for life in the future. The greatest daring lies, rather, in the fact that a human creature, made out of the dust of the earth, should stake everything on love as the foundation of being, here and now. But if any man would know it thoroughly in his own experience he must needs give up his dependence, his role, his judgment of himself, his despair, and his possessions in order that he may finally establish the self upon the eternal foundation of loving and being loved.

"WHEN I AWAKE"

See now how the sublime epic of redemption and of eternal life leads to completeness. The human creature, born of nature, can

love if he is loved. In earliest life the love which he receives and
that which he gives are good beyond all other human graces, yet
that love, whether received or given, is always tinged with im-
perfection, that is, it is not perfect, not complete. The Christian
symbols of salvation through Jesus Christ raise the meaning of being loved to a cosmic and eternal plane; for these symbols show
perfect love coming forth eternally from God toward the human
creature. These symbols pledge that God will supply the perfect
love which it is beyond any human creature's capacity to give.

So, too, the Christian symbols concerning human faith raise the
meaning of loving in response, to that same plane of eternal significance. By loving in response to love poured out, the human
creature, born of nature, is now born "of the Spirit." And thus
faith which is love given in response to God shades imperceptibly
into the results of that faith, which is the substance, that is to say,
the reality, of eternal life in the present.

At every stage throughout life man is confronted in some manner by the living God, in the common crises of ordinary life. In
each such confrontation the human soul is challenged to growth
and further maturity. And at every stage he can go forward in
faith, or shrink back in unbelief.

Then as the human drama draws toward its close, a man is moving toward his final and most profound confrontation which is not
death but life, life in transition. The Christian symbols concerning this unending life represent it as a life of unimaginable completeness, unimaginable because we have nothing with which to
compare it; or else, a life of continuing deterioration.

The "I am," which is the human soul, knows itself about to
encounter, not a nothingness, but the "I am" who is God. And if
one has been able to simplify the soul to its depths so that love is
the foundation and essence of its being, that soul is at one with God.
There is no need for a frantic unburdening of cargo as if preparing
for a storm. That disburdening of the soul has already been done
in the process of simplification.

Then it is as if the soul, already well at home in eternal life, should some day slip quietly away, "from out our bourne of time and place," and sail into the sunrise. And the going is not an hour for sorrow, but rather for gladness. For the soul knows that it is not, and will never be, alone.

Notes

CHAPTER ONE

1 Hebrews 7:16.
2 Sherrill, L. J., *Guilt and Redemption*, Chapter VII (Richmond, John Knox Press, 1945), gives detailed evidence for these general statements.
3 Among recent publications dealing with stages of the human life span, indebtedness is acknowledged to Josselyn, Irene M., *Psychosocial Development of Children* (New York Family Service Association of America, 1948), and Adler, Gerhard, *Studies in Analytical Psychology* (New York: W. W. Norton, 1948).
4 Genesis 11:31 f.
5 Genesis, Chapter 28.
6 Isaiah, Chapter 6.
7 Ezekiel 24:15 f.
8 Acts, Chapter 9.
9 Judges, Chapter 13.
10 Genesis 50:20.
(all quotations from the American Standard Version are used by permission of the International Council of Religious Education)
11 Hebrews 10:38, A.S.V.
12 Hebrews 3:18, 19, A.S.V.
13 Hebrews 10:37–39, A.S.V.
14 Hebrews 11:1.
15 Hebrews 8:5; 9:23.
16 Hebrews 8:5.
17 Hebrews 9:9.
18 Hebrews 11:1; 1:3.
19 Hebrews 11:1.
20 Hebrews 1:3.
21 Hebrews 1:3.
22 Hebrews 1:3.
23 Hebrews 9:11–15.
24 Hebrews 11:1.
25 John 3:3, A.S.V.
26 Matthew 10:34.

CHAPTER TWO

1 Isaiah 9:6, italics supplied.
2 Genesis 2:15 f.
3 Hinsie, L. E., *The Person in the Body*, Chapter 5 (New York: W. W. Norton & Co., 1945).
4 Genesis 21:6; Job 5:22; 8:21; Luke 6:21.
5 Luke 2:46–55.
6 In Galatians 4:26 Paul writes: "Jerusalem which is above, is free, which is the mother of us all." Apparently the most that can be claimed for this as a reference to the church would be to say that it refers to what is sometimes called "the church invisible," that is, the perfect, eternal church, but not the church as a visible society in the here and now.

CHAPTER THREE

[1] Genesis 2:24.

[2] Terman, L. M., *Psychological Factors in Marital Happiness* (New York, McGraw-Hill, 1938); Burgess, E. W., and Cottrell, L. S., *Predicting Success or Failure in Marriage* (New York, Prentice-Hall, 1939).

[3] Gilmore, Harlan W., "Five Generations of a Begging Family," *American Journal of Sociology*, March, 1932, pp. 768 f.

[4] For a study of the way in which social stratification affects youth, see Hollingshead, A. B., *Elmtown's Youth* (New York, John Wiley & Sons, 1949).

[5] Compare the characterizing phrase, "the idea of redemption through progress," Niebuhr, Reinhold, *Faith and History*, Chapter I (New York, Charles Scribner's Sons, 1949).

[6] Luke 2:51.

CHAPTER FOUR

[1] Dostoyevsky, F., *The Brothers Karamazov*, Book VI, Chapter 2 (First Modern Library Edn., 1929, pp. 375-376).

[2] Bergler, Edmund, *Unhappy Marriage and Divorce*, *passim* (New York International University Press, 1946).

CHAPTER FIVE

[1] Moloney, J. C., *The Magic Cloak, A Contribution to the Psychology of Authoritarianism*, Chapter 8 (Wakefield, Mass., The Montrose Press, 1949).

[2] *E.g.*, Papini, G., *Saint Augustine*, Chapter 2 (New York, Harcourt Brace & Co., 1930).

[3] Fife, R. H., *Young Luther*, Chapter 1 (New York, The Macmillan Co., 1928).

[4] *Cf.* Durant, W., *The Story of Philosophy*, p. 326 f. (New revised edition, New York, Garden City Publishing Co., 1938).

[5] *Cf.* Kuhn, Helmut, "Existentialism —Christian and Anti-Christian," *Theology Today*, October, 1949, pp. 211 f.

[6] Wallace, W., *Life of Arthur Schopenhauer*, Chapters 2, 3, 7 (London, 1890).

[7] Kuhn, op. cit.

[8] Kierkegaard, S., *The Sickness unto Death*, translated by W. Lowrie, p. 17 (Princeton, Princeton University Press, 1941, used by permission).

[9] Lowrie, W., *Kierkegaard*, Chapter 1 (Oxford University Press, London, 1938).

[10] Swenson, D. F., *Something About Kierkegaard*, Chapter 1 (Minneapolis, Augsburg Publishing House, 1941).

[11] Kuhn, H., *Encounter with Nothingness* (Hinsdale, Ill., Henry Regnery, 1949).

[12] Exodus, Chapter 3.

CHAPTER SIX

[1] Bureau of the Census, "Forecast of the Population of the United States, 1945–1975," pages 47, 51, 67 (Washington, 1945).

[2] I Timothy 6:7.

[3] Maves, P. E. and Cedarleaf, J. L., *Older People and the Church*, Chapter 7 (Copyright 1949 by Pierce and Smith). By permission of Abingdon-Cokesbury Press.

[4] Maves and Cedarleaf, *op. cit.*, pp. 137–141 (Used by permission of Abingdon-Cokesbury Press, New York).

[5] Jerome, *Commentariorum in Epistolam ad Galatas*, Lib. III, Cap. vi:10—in Migne, *Patrologia Latina*, Vol. 26, Col. 433.

[6] *Cf.* Lawrence, W., *Life of Phillips Brooks*, Chapter 6 (New York, Harper and Bros., 1930).

[7] Hutton, J. A., *Finally: with Paul to the End* (New York, Harper and Bros., n.d.).

[8] Oates, W. E., *The Diagnostic Use of the Bible* (unpublished paper).

[9] Col. 3:12–15, R.E.V.